D0621520

The Basilica of
St. Mark in Venice

The Basilica of
St. Mark in Venice

edited by
ETTORE VIO

SCALA

THE BASILICA OF ST. MARK IN VENICE
edited by *Ettore Vio*

Authors of the texts
Prof. Ennio Concina, *director of the department of art history at the IUAV*
Dr. Umberto Daniele, *art historian*
Dr. Maria da Villa Urbani, *chief librarian of the Basilica*
Mgr. Antonio Niero, *procurator of St. Mark and instructor in history at Ca' Foscari University*
Prof. Guido Tigler, *instructor in history of art at Florence University*
Arch. Ettore Vio, proto *of St. Mark and responsible for the conservation of the Basilica*
Prof. Licia Vlad Borrelli, *chief inspector of the Ministry of Cultural Assets*

Editorial coordination and graphic design
Andrea Grandese

Editing
Patrizia Bevilacqua

Video paging
Colophon srl, Venice

Translation
Huw Evans

Photographs
Archivio Fotografico SCALA (M. Falsini, M. Sarri, Cameraphoto) except: pages 9, 34, 66, 69, 91, 143 (Cameraphoto) and pages 19, 56, 58, 62, 112, 135, 152, 153 (Procuratoria di San Marco).

The drawings on pages 29, 50, 54, 56, 59, 77, 78, 94-5, 97, 145 and 166 have been kindly provided by the Procuratoria di San Marco and the architect Ettore Vio.

The axonometric projections on page 89, drawn by Ettore Vio, are taken from the book *San Marco. I mosaici. La storia. L'illuminazione*, Fabbri Editore, 1990.

1999 SCALA, Istituto Fotografico Editoriale
Antella (Florence)
Printed in Italy

All rights reserved.
Reproduction in any form is forbidden without the written permission of the publisher.

ISBN 88-8117-276-3

Contents

History and Art

9 St. Mark's: a Biographical Profile

21 Liturgy in St. Mark's: the Mosaics and the Rites

35 The Art of St. Mark's

Tour of the Basilica

51 The Tour of the Basilica

53 The Exterior of the Basilica

66 The Gothic Decoration of the Copings

68 The Arches of the Central Portal

70 The Horses of St. Mark

77 The Narthex

86 The Mosaics

90 The Porta da Mar

93 The Interior of the Basilica

108 The Iconostasis of the Dalle Masegne Brothers

110 The Baldachin

114 The Inscriptions of the Mosaics

134 The Tessellated Floor of St. Mark's

142 The Crypt

145 The Chapels

152 The Inlaid Cabinets in the Sacristy

154 The Angels in the Baptistery

158 The Mosaics of the Mascoli Chapel

163 The Pala d'oro and the Treasury of St. Mark's

173 The Tapestries

174 Essential Bibliography

HISTORY AND ART

St. Mark's: a Biographical Profile

Antonio Niero

The evangelist Mark first stepped onto the stage of history in the year 43 or 44, when the apostle Peter, after escaping from prison in miraculous fashion, took refuge in "the house of Mary, the mother of John, whose surname was Mark" (Acts of the Apostles, 12, 12). Double names like this were not uncommon in Jewish circles at the time. The first and strictly theophoric name (*Yohanan*) meant "god is gracious" in Hebrew, whereas the second (*Marcus*) was a Roman name derived from the god Mars and used by prosperous clans, although for Tertullian (*c.* 200 AD) it had almost become a common noun, corresponding roughly to our "fellow," "person." It was to the house of Mary and John Mark that the apostle Saul, as he was then still known, and his friend Barnabas, born in Cyprus and a relative of Mark's (whether an uncle or a cousin, we don't know) went in the early months of 45. They brought with them a substantial collection raised by the Christian community of Antioch to aid that of Jerusalem, which found itself in straitened circumstances as a consequence of the food shortages from which the Roman empire had been suffering for years. The young and now fatherless Mark was probably born a few decades after Jesus. There is a lively passage in his Gospel (14, 51-2) which is thought to be linked to his own life. In a few, brief lines, it describes a dramatic nocturnal scene. While the soldiers arrested Jesus in the garden in the dead of night, a young man wrapped in a linen cloth suddenly appeared, following the Master. The soldiers, unhappy with the presence of an inconvenient witness, laid hold of him, perhaps to find out who he was. But the young man instinctively slipped off the linen cloth and fled from them, naked. A number of scholars have interpreted this passage as a reference to the evangelist himself, serving as a sort of signature to his Gospel. Analysis of some of the details suggests that he came from a middle-class family, for only the well-to-do could afford linen. The presumed affluence of the anonymous young man would fit in well with the references in the Acts to the house of Mark's mother Mary, where the early Christian community in Jerusalem used to gather after the ascension of Christ. According to the Acts again (12, 25), Saul and Barnabas took John Mark with them when they returned to Antioch from Jerusalem, a journey that may have been made at the beginning of 46. It is likely that Barnabas had chosen the young man as a companion because of their kinship. Given his

1

West façade. Mosaic on the bowl-shaped vault of the portal of St. Alypius, 13th century, detail

2

Paolino da Venezia, plan of the city, drawn after Tommaso Temanza from the parchment codex *Chronologia magna* of 1376

The bounds of the ducal *castrum-castellum* in the area of St. Mark's are indicated by a battlemented enclosure. It was inside this that the first church of St. Mark, the Palatine chapel, was built between 829 and 832 AD to house the body of the saint.

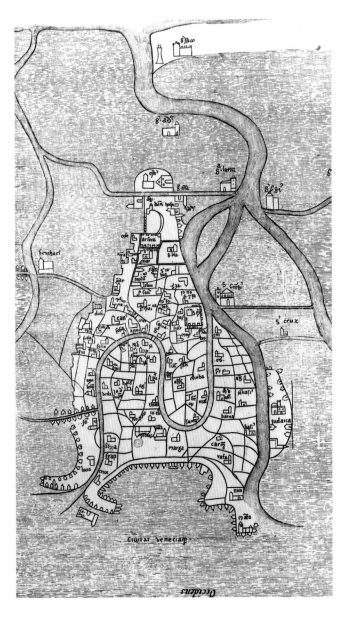

plans to return to the island of his birth to preach the Gospel, he probably thought his fairly quick and alert young relative would come in useful as a secretary, diarist and general assistant. The other companion, though one of quite different stature, was Saul. In any case, the missionaries left the populous, wealthy and corrupt city, bathed by the Orontes River, after a dramatic meeting briefly outlined in the Acts (13, 2). The prophets and teachers of the local Christian community were told by the Holy Spirit: "Separate me Barnabas and Saul for the work whereunto I have called them." And the Acts continue (13, 4): "So they, being sent forth by the Holy Ghost, departed unto Seleucia; and from thence they sailed to Cyprus." Seleucia, Antioch's port, was some twenty-five kilometers from the city. The sea crossing was fairly quick, perhaps taking barely twenty-four hours.

They landed at Salamis, the main port, largest city and former capital of the island, where the Jewish colony, in existence for over two centuries, had many synagogues (Acts, 13, 5). At this point in the account John Mark is officially recognized as their assistant. The three missionaries set about preaching the Gospel in the local synagogues. However, Salamis was just a stage on their journey. The final goal was the capital Paphos, on the other, western side of the island. Before reaching there the three men had to cross the whole island (Acts, 13, 6). We do not know what route they took: through the mountains of the interior or along the coast road to the south that led to New Paphos. It was from here that the Roman proconsul Sergius Paulus governed the island. As he had the reputation of being a learned man and interested in spiritual matters, the missionaries felt that his conversion, or at least his support,

would help Christianity to gain a foothold on Cyprus. And in fact Sergius Paulus was an astonished witness to the dramatic clash between Saul and the sorcerer Bar-Jesus, also known as Elymas, who was half scholar and half soothsayer and claimed to be an intermediary between God and human beings. But Bar-Jesus, who tried to turn the proconsul away from Saul's preaching, was temporarily blinded by the apostle. It is from this moment that he is always referred to as Paul (Acts, 13, 9-12). This made such an impression on the proconsul that he converted to Christianity. Indeed, it seems that he counseled the preachers to leave Cyprus and head for the heart of Asia Minor (modern-day Turkey), to preach the Gospel at Antioch in Pisidia. The missionaries set sail again, perhaps in the spring of 47, and after a brief crossing landed at the port of Attalia, in Pamphylia on the coast of Asia Minor. From here they traveled inland, up river or by foot along the road that ran alongside it, with the intention of crossing the forbidding mountains of the Taurus. But at Perga, in the foothills, Mark suddenly decided to leave his two friends and return to Jerusalem (Acts, 13, 13). This was the famous crisis of Perga, and debate over the reasons for Mark's decision has raged since the early days of Christianity. He may have been motivated by a desire to see his mother again, or perhaps he was not happy with the fact that Paul had become the leader of the mission instead of his relative Barnabas.

But Mark had not broken off all relations with the two missionaries. He made contact with them again after the apostolic council held at Jerusalem in 49, when he met his friends again at Antioch. On this occasion Barnabas proposed to Paul that Mark should accompany them on a second and

3

Saint Mark on His Way to Alexandria, mosaic, 13th century, Zen Chapel

The detail showing the saint traveling to Alexandria, where he would be made bishop and martyred around 68 AD, is part of the mosaics representing *Scenes from the Life of St. Mark.*

4

Saint Mark Healing Anian, mosaic, 13th century, Zen Chapel

The mosaic is one of the "panels" with scenes from the life of the saint that adorn the ceiling of the chapel, formerly the *Porta da Mar,* through which Venetians landing at the wharf used to enter the church to pay their respects to St. Mark.

longer apostolic journey. But Paul was unshakable in his refusal, leading to a fierce clash of words with Barnabas, for he regarded Mark as a weakling, not to say a traitor, since he had abandoned them at Perga. But this time Barnabas was adamant in defense of his kinsman and broke off his long friendship and cooperation with Paul. The latter chose Silas as his new companion and left Asia Minor for the distant shores of Europe. Barnabas and Mark were left with no alternative but to retrace their previous journey and return to the island of Cyprus, something they were quite happy to do (Acts, 15, 37-41). From here on the Acts have nothing further to say on the subject. There is an apocryphal text of no historical validity whatsoever, the so-called *Acts of Barnabas* dating from the fourth century, whose account of the two missionaries' adventures in the land of Cyprus is crammed with fantastic episodes, fabulous deeds and tales bordering on the ridiculous. For reliable information about Mark we have to go back to the texts of the New Testament. By 54, Mark must have been

back in Paul's good graces, if it is true that the latter, writing to his friend Philemon of Colossae, did not omit to send his greetings to Mark. Paul was to have need of Mark in some of the most difficult moments of his life, such as the time of his second imprisonment in Rome, assuming that the references to the evangelist in the Letters to the Colossians and in the second Letter to Timothy are really his own work and not that of his school, and therefore written after his death. In the meantime Mark had become Peter's assistant in Rome, once again if we are to accept that the mention of him by the apostle at the end of the first Letter (5, 13) is his and should not instead be attributed to a late follower writing shortly before 100. Mark's collaboration with Peter is given a sounder basis if we look at evidence from outside the Bible, such as that provided by the ecclesiastic writers active between the second and fourth century. If we are to accept the claims made in the works of St. Irenaeus and St. Clement, both writing around 200, Mark had transcribed the sermons given by Peter

5 *left*

Saint Mark Writing His Gospel, mosaic, 13th century, Zen Chapel

The mosaic is one of the "panels" with scenes from the life of the saint that adorn the ceiling of the chapel, formerly the *Porta da Mar.*

6 *facing page*

The Saint Ordained Bishop, mosaic, 12th century, left-hand choir of the presbytery

The walls and ceilings of the two choirs, so-called because they are still used to house the organs and the choristers that accompany sacred services, are adorned with scenes from the life of the patron saint.

7 *following pages*

Saint Mark Dragged through the City and Burial of the Saint, mosaic, 13th century, Zen Chapel

The mosaics belong to the "panels" with scenes from the life of the saint that adorn the ceiling of the chapel, formerly the *Porta da Mar.* In fact they are the last two, in which the images are accompanied by the inscriptions "here he is dragged in chains toward the locality of Bucoli" and "St. Mark is buried by the followers of Christ."

in Rome at the urging of members of the Roman social and military classes and with the approval of the apostle himself. In practice, this must be a reference to Mark's Gospel (written prior to the year 70), the second of the four according to tradition from St. Augustine onward. This Gospel is a masterpiece in miniature, the shortest of the four, made up of no more than sixteen chapters in the Greek tongue. It shows a distinct preference for the story of Christ's life, insisting on the details and in particular the events that took place around the sea of Galilee, so that St. Mark's Gospel could be described as a "Gospel of the Sea." Mark also refers to the open countryside and scattered villages of the land around Galilee. Above all, however, he speaks of the crowd, at times vast, that almost always assailed the Messiah in a desperate attempt to cure themselves of all sorts of ailments or free themselves of possession by devils, or simply to hear the good word. In essence Mark set out to demonstrate, through the recounting of numerous miracles, that Jesus was indeed the Son of God. In his turn, Eusebius of Caesarea, the greatest historian of the ancient Church, wrote around 300 that Mark founded the Church of Alexandria, organizing it on a parochial basis, but he did not go into specific detail. After Eusebius, local tradition built up a history of Mark's deeds in Africa, as an apostle first in Cyrenaica and then in Alexandria, up until his martyrdom on April 25 of what was probably the year 68. From the archeological viewpoint, what we do know is that there was a tomb of St. Mark at Boucolis, an eastern suburb of Alexandria on the Mediterranean coast, in the fifth century. And that the relics of the saint were moved from place to place in the Alexandrine region several times over the course of the centuries, before returning to Boucolis in the seventh century. It was from here that, around 828, two traders from the Venetian lagoons, Buono da Malamocco and Rustico da Torcello, managed to carry off the body of the saint by means

of a cunning stratagem. They had learned from the custodians of Mark's sanctuary in Boucolis that it was to be destroyed on the orders of the Arab governor of Alexandria and its marble used to build a palace at Al-Fustat, once called Babylon. To avert such desecration the two merchants offered to carry the remains of the evangelist to safety in Venice. Faced with reluctance on the part of the custodians, who advanced a series of objections, not least the saint's patronage of the city, the merchants pointed out that St. Mark, before going to found the Church in Alexandria, had been sent by the apostle Paul to preach to the Veneti. Indeed they argued that Mark, caught in a storm in the marshes where Venice now stands while on his way back to Rome with Hermagoras of Aquileia, whom he had chosen as his successor and bishop, had received a heavenly vision that his body would not perish after death, but was destined instead for eternal repose and veneration in Venice. Though unwilling, the custodians agreed to the merchants' request, though not without trying to pull a fast one on them by substituting the remains of the martyred St. Claudia for those of Mark. Hiding the sacred relics under layers of pork meat, which the Muslim customs officers of Alexandria found repulsive, they were able to smuggle them out by declaring, when the time came for inspection, that what they were carrying was indeed *kanzir*, i.e. pork. They were allowed to leave the port and after an adventurous voyage across the Mediterranean and up the Adriatic, with halts at Cropani in Calabria, Zara in Dalmatia and Umago in Istria, the navigators reached Venice, sending news of their precious cargo ahead to Doge Giustiniano Parteciaco. When they landed in Venice the doge and his court, along with the local bishop and clergy, came to meet the bold adventurers. St. Mark's body, received with great pomp and ceremony, was placed in a corner of the doge's palace until such time as a suitable basilica could be built to house it. This took place on January 31, 828, according to later tradition.

Yet we have to ask how much truth there was in the claims about St. Mark's Venetian apostolate that the merchants used to persuade the custodians of Mark's tomb in Alexandria to hand over the sacred relics. Recent studies have shown that it was in fact a legend, which grew up over the course of the seventh century and was gradually amplified until it took on the form in which it appears in Doge Andrea Dandolo's *Chronica*, written in the middle of the fourteenth century.

8 *preceding pages*

West façade. Mosaic on the bowl-shaped vault of the portal of St. Alypius, 13th century

The doge, accompanied by the clergy and the people, brings the sarcophagus containing the saint's body into the church. This is the earliest picture of the basilica in its resplendent new guise of marble and columns imported from the East, with the domes raised and covered in lead and the four horses already placed on the terrace. The date is between 1265 and 1270.

9

Antonio Visentini, St. Mark's Basilica, Section through the Baptistery, engraving, 18th century

The print shows the wooden structures of the domes and the rooms above the atrium. Visentini made this engraving of the basilica in the eighteen twenties. The artist took a scientific approach, investigating structures and parts of the basilica that were little known and frequented.

The small basilica in the form of a martyrium, erected in Venice to house the body of St. Mark, became one of the most famous Christian sanctuaries of the early Middle Ages, drawing pilgrims from all over Europe. Damaged by the fire which broke out in August 976 and destroyed several areas of the city, it was quickly repaired by Doge Pietro Orseolo. Less than a century later, in 1063, Doge Domenico Contarini decided to demolish St. Mark's sanctuary and replace it with a larger and richer basilica, the present building with its five domes designed – it is supposed – by an anonymous Byzantine architect. The work did not proceed rapidly. It was not until 1094 that the building was finished, during the reign of Doge Vitale Falier. It was he who decided to have it consecrated, so that it could also serve as a palatine chapel or dogal church, annexed to the city's seat of government. The bishop of Venice, Enrico Contarini, was invited to conduct the ceremony. But when the time came to transfer St. Mark's body to the new building, it proved impossible to find. Many explanations were put forward, not least that it had been consumed in the fire of 976, or that the location of its burial place had been forgotten. Prayers and days of fasting were proclaimed. In the end, on June 25, while the doge, bishop, nobility and populace gathered in prayer and lamentation in

the basilica, one of St. Mark's arms emerged from a pillar on the southern side of the temple to indicate that his body rested there. It was true. The sacred relics were then placed at the center of the building, this time steeped in the sweet scent of roses. News of the discovery spread rapidly through the Veneto region and the rest of Europe. More and more pilgrims came to visit the holy relics, among them nobles, common people and even the Holy Roman Emperor, encouraged by a series of miracles wrought by the saint, some of which caused a great stir. On October 8 the body, housed in a precious sarcophagus, was placed inside the crypt that had been built by Doge Falier. Here it remained until the first half of the nineteenth century when, to make it easier for the faithful to show their devotion, it was moved to a new location under the table of the high altar, where it still lies today. To such an extent did the relics become the symbol of Venice and its government that the Florentine man of letters Angelo Fiorenzuola (1493-1543) was moved to write, in his *Ragionamenti d'amore*, that the saint was honored more highly in Venice than God himself.

Liturgy in St. Mark's: the Mosaics and the Rites

Antonio Niero

In the 8000 square meters of mosaic that cover the inside and outside of the basilica it is possible to discern an underlying iconographic program drawn up by an anonymous Venetian scholar, perhaps the theologian Iacobo Venetico Greco, a canon of the basilica who was active around 1136.

It is true that, prior to the modern hypotheses on the subject, the program had been ascribed since the late fifteenth century to Joachim of Fiore (c. 1145-1202), the charismatic abbot of a Cistercian monastery in the Calabrian region of Aspromonte. It was said that he had come to St. Mark's and drawn up the entire scheme for the mosaic. Today it is difficult to find support for such a hypothesis, although some illustrious scholars, including most recently the Viennese Otto Demus, do not exclude the possibility of Joachim's involvement at some stage. While it is possible to discern signs of the influence of Joachim's work (in the figures of *Virtues* in the dome of the Ascension, in the four Biblical rivers in its pendentives, in some details of the *Cycle of the Passion and Resurrection* and in the monks in the aisles of the dome of the Pentecost), we can divide the mosaics in St. Mark's from the strict viewpoint of their content into themes taken from the Bible and those drawn from the lives of the saints. The biblical themes, in turn, are split between those from the Old Testament, arranged in strictly chronological order in the atrium that runs round three sides of the basilica, and those from the New Testament, located inside. There are just two exceptions to this: the *Scenes*

10

Detail of the right-hand ambo called the pergolo grando

The ambo, made out of splendid plutei of imperial red granite supported by nine columns in antique breccia, is hexagonal and is located in the doge's part of the church. It was used for the presentation of the doge to the people after his election.

11

Cain and Abel, mosaic, 12th century, chapel of St. Clement

Set around the window from which the doge was able to attend Mass, the mosaic does not fit into any of the classical iconographies and constitutes an admonition to the doge. The inscription "Christ has respect unto Abel, but unto Cain and his offering he has not respect" (Gen. 4,4) warns that all of the doge's actions must be disinterested and transparent.

from the Story of Susanna and Daniel, set on the left, above the wall at the entrance to the Nikopoia Chapel, and a fragment of the *Sacrifice of Cain and Abel* (all that is left of a larger mosaic decorating the balcony from where the doge and his wife attended daily Mass up until at least the fourteenth century) on the right, in the chapel of San Clemente.

In all likelihood the mosaics in the atrium were begun in 1230, following the rebuilding of the structure after its destruction in an earthquake. They follow a scheme based on the choral liturgy, according to the rite of the Roman Curia that derived from the reform carried out by the Franciscan Aymon of Faversham between 1243 and 1244. The use of this liturgy at St. Mark's is documented in the contemporary *Antiphonal* published by Cattin (*Musica e liturgia a San Marco*, II, Venice 1990). The liturgical sequence commenced with Septuagesima and then continued with Sexagesima, Quinquagesima and the Sundays of Lent. The reading of the *Creation of the World* commenced on Septuagesima, the third Sunday before Lent. This was followed by the *Story of Noah* at Sexagesima and that of Abraham at Quinquagesima. On the first Sunday in Lent the reading of the biblical text was omitted, its place taken by a text from the writings of the Fathers of the Church. The Bible returned on the following Sundays with the *Story of Isaac and Jacob* (second Sunday), with the tale of how Joseph was sold by his brothers, became a high-ranking official of the Pharaoh and was recognized by them when they came to Egypt (third Sunday) and with the story of how Moses freed his people from enslavement to the

12 *preceding pages*
Scenes from the Story of Noah, Judgment and Burial of Noah, mosaic, 13th century, western atrium
Noah is shown sleeping naked after drinking wine made from the vine he had planted after the Flood; his sons Shem and Japheth, watched by Ham, cover up their father's nakedness while walking backward. Waking, Noah predicts that Ham will be his brothers' servant. He was buried at the age of 950.

13
Scenes from the Story of Joseph and His Brothers, mosaic, 13th century, western atrium, first cupola of Joseph
Joseph recounts a dream to his brothers: a premonition that he will be great one day. To rid themselves of him, his envious brothers first lower him into a well and then sell him as a slave to Midianite traders, who take him to Egypt.

Pharaoh and led them across the Red Sea (fourth Sunday). These themes are all represented in mosaic, starting from the far right-hand side of the atrium, on the inside of its domes and on the walls, and proceeding along the northern arm with the *Scenes from the Lives of Joseph and Moses*. The mosaics are based on the biblical texts. They have been continued, independently of the liturgical order, in an anthological manner so as to fill the spaces of the walls, which would otherwise have been left blank. Usually each story occupies a single dome. Only that of Joseph extends over three domes. A variety of interpretations have been given to this exception. One possibility is that greater space was given to the tale of Joseph, which is narrated moreover with superb artistic skill, as a mark of honor to the official of Pharaonic Egypt, the land converted to Christianity by St. Mark and the place from where his body was brought to Venice.

In some scenes it is possible to detect signs of Venetian nationalism. In the representation of the creation of the animals, for instance, in the second circle of the first dome on the right, the first creatures to prostrate themselves in worship before God are a pair of lions, symbol of the republic, in an apparent sign of divine predestination. In the *Scenes from the Flood*, the Ark contains not only peacocks, symbol of the Persian empire, and eagles, alluding to the Byzantine empire, but also lions, a reference both to the kingdom of Judah and the republic of Venice, its ideal heir. On the plane of the iconographic sources, there is now general acceptance of the arguments put forward by the Finnish scholar Tikkanen, who holds that the mosaicists in the atrium took their inspiration largely from the *Cotton Bible*, a biblical codex of Egyptian origin dating from the reign of Constantine and now in a British museum, while those who represented the *Scenes from the Life of Moses* were influenced by the so-called *Gerona Bible* from the time of the revival brought about by the Paleologus dynasty after 1261.

14

Scenes from the Story of Moses, mosaic, 13th century, north atrium, lunette above the Porta dei Fiori

The scene represents the miracle of the manna: "in the morning fell manna, and after quails fell too." The next scene is that of the water flowing from the rock: "Moses smites the rock a second time and water flows for the people in abundance."

The mosaic decoration of the atrium was completed around 1275. That of the interior, on the other hand, was commenced as soon as the basilica was finished, i.e. shortly after 1094, and work on it continued up until 1204, though it is now recognized that some of the mosaics were executed as late as the middle of the century.

According to a suggestive hypothesis put forward by Demus, and one founded on their actual topographical arrangement, the mosaics of the interior are a development of the so-called *historia salutis*, along the longitudinal axis starting from the dome of the presbytery, or dome of the Emmanuel, the envoy of the Eternal Father eagerly-awaited by the peoples (whence the name dome of the Father), more or less as far as the *Time of Advent* and of Christmas and Epiphany. The following mosaics, to the right and left, are roughly based on the passages from the Gospels used on the Sundays after Epiphany and on weekdays during Lent. Exemplary, in this connection, are the extremely elegant mosaics on the right drawn from the Gospel text of the first Sunday of Lent and representing the *Temptations of Jesus*. These are followed by scenes from the *Passion*, *Death*, *Resurrection* and *Ascension*, in the mosaics on the right- and left-hand walls and of the *Triumph of Christ* in the second dome, or dome of the Ascension. The period after Easter was dominated by readings from the Acts of the Apostles. These are represented in the space of the lateral tribunes in front of the dome of the Pentecost, where the stories of the twelve apostles are narrated, drawing on reliable historical sources as well as on apocryphal writings. The text of Revelation, the last book in the Bible and final chapter in the history of the human race, is depicted between the third dome, or dome of Pentecost, and the way out of the basilica. The other liturgical cycles on a smaller scale are those of the Holy Communion and the life of Mary. At least from the middle of the fourteenth century up until 1517, the receptacle of the Eucharist was located on the wall to the left of the entrance to the presbytery, as was the custom at the time. As a consequence the surrounding mosaics center on the mystery of Communion, in terms either of its prefiguration in the Old Testament or of its institution in the New Testament. Above the staircase leading to the receptacle are set the majestic figures of Moses and Elijah with eucharistic inscriptions, while the wall opposite is decorated with scenes from the Gospel story of the centurion praying for his ailing servant, *Domine*

non sum dignus..., echoed in the liturgy of the Mass at the moment of Communion, as well as the *Last Supper*, which is given a clearly eucharistic significance by the presence of a dog, a specific late-medieval symbol. The extensive treatment of the story of the supper at Emmaus on the upper side of the Nikopoia Chapel is connected with these scenes. The Marian cycle, on the other hand, is laid out fanwise on the two western walls of the transept and terminates in the middle of the atrium. The *Scenes from the Birth of the Virgin*, based on the apocryphal texts (the *Protevangelium of James*) are represented on the first, where the emphasis is placed on episodes involving the Virgin's parents, Joachim and Anne, while the scenes from the *Childhood of Mary*, the *Marriage to Joseph* and the *Annunciation* appear on the opposite wall on the right. The Marian theme is taken up again in the *Death of the Virgin*, located in the so-called well in the middle of the atrium, in a partially Byzantine scheme that places the story of Mary alongside the Christological one of the *historia salutis*. The two representations of the sources of revelation, i.e. the Holy Scriptures and the Tradition of the Doctors of the Church, in

15

General plan of the basilica showing the location of the principal mosaics

1. west atrium	**13**. tribune of the	procurators
2. north atrium	Madonna of the Kiss	**26**. east vault of the
3. baptistery	**14**. Mascoli Chapel	Ascension and
4. vault of the	**15**. chapel of	iconostasis
Apocalypse	St. Isidore	**27**. tribune of the
5. tribune of	**16**. dome of St. John	patriarch
St. Peter	**17**. north vault of	**28**. altar of the
6. tribune of the	the Ascension	Blessed Virgin
Three Saints or	**18**. dome of the	Nikopoia
St. Clement	Ascension	**29**. chapel of
7. dome of Pentecost	**19**. south vault of	St. Peter
or the Holy Spirit	the Ascension	**30**. presbytery
8. north vault of	**20**. dome of	**31**. dome of the
Pentecost	St. Leonard	choir or the
9. south vault of	**21**. treasury	Prophets or the
Pentecost	**22**. sanctuary	Emmanuel
10. west vault of the	**23**. altar of	**32**. chapel of
Ascension	St. Leonard	St. Clement
11. capital of the	**24**. pier of the	**33**. apse with Christ
Crucifix	Finding of	the Pantocrator
12. Madonna of the	Saint Mark	**34**. sacristy
Rifle	**25**. tribune of the	

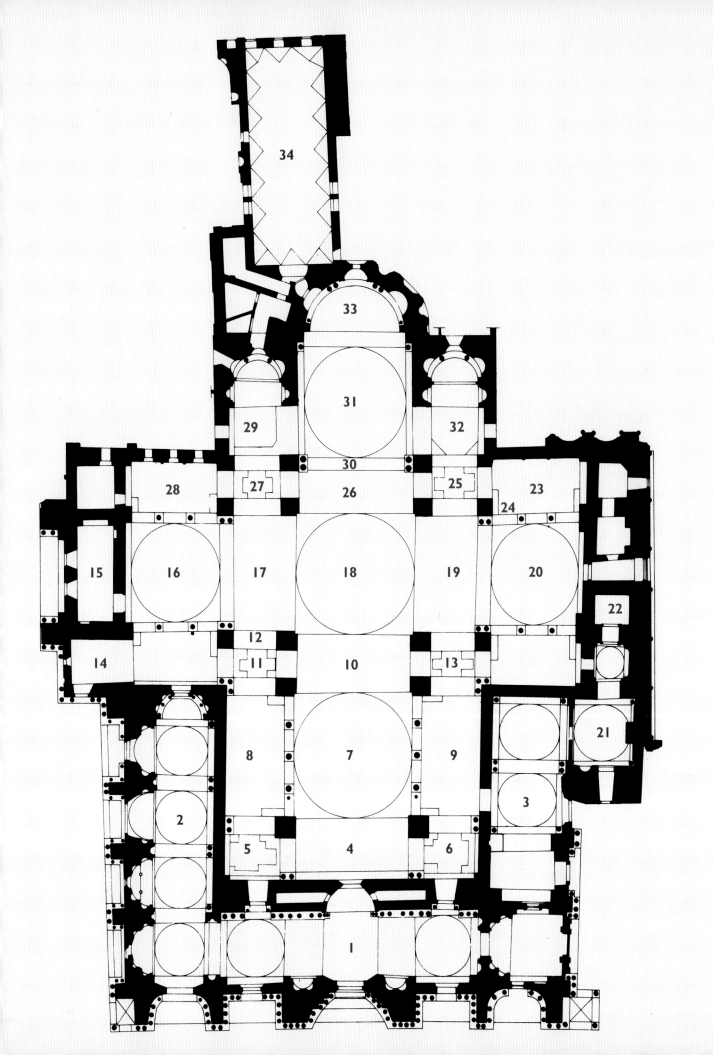

the pendentives of the dome of the Ascension and of the next one to the north, the dome of St. John the Evangelist, should be seen in relation to these liturgical themes. Today theology, after the Second Vatican Council, admits the union of Holy Scriptures and Tradition as the sole source of divine revelation, whereas in classical doctrine, and in particular that of the Middle Ages, the two sources were regarded as distinct. In fact the presence of the four evangelists and the rivers of the Garden of Eden associated with them in the pendentives of the domes of the Ascension is intended to show that divine revelation flows to the Church and to humanity through the written Word of God, or Holy Scripture. In the pendentives of the dome of St. John the Evangelist, on the other hand, we find the four classical Doctors of the Western Church, i.e. Ambrose, Augustine, Gregory the Great and Jerome, alluding to Tradition. The interaction between Holy Scripture and Tradition is also reflected on the outside of the basilica, in the statues at the top of the north front representing the four Doctors of the Church and the ones on the west and main façade, depicting the four Evangelists.

We now come to the cycles of scenes from the lives of the saints. Whether arranged to form a *continuum historicum*, as in the case of St. Mark, the Apostle Peter, the other apostles and St. John the Evangelist in particular, as well as Pope Clement I and St. Leonard of Limoges, or isolated images, they make up a total of 181 figures. The presence of many of these saints can be connected with the political and trade links established by the republic with markets in the East and West, as with St. Leonard (France) and St. Boniface (the German-speaking lands).

Numerous religious festivals were held in the basilica and are recorded in the *Ordo*, i.e. the specific liturgical calendar. Four feast days were devoted to the patron saint, Mark: January 31, commemorating the translation of his body; April 25, the day of his martyrdom; June 25, the day on which his relics were found; and October 8, in memory of the dedication of the basilica. On January 31 the city's clergy walked in procession around the saint's altar, to the sound of psalms. Since the early part of the nineteenth century and right up to the present day, the feast of April 25 has commonly been called *San Marco dei bocoli*, "St. Mark of the Buds," after the custom of presenting a rosebud to your beloved or to women in general. The other festivals have also been given popular

names, in use since at least the early seventeenth century. That of January 31 was known as *San Marco dei mezéni*, in memory of the fact that the saint's relics had been transported to Venice concealed in the middle (*in mezzo*, whence the name) of layers of pork (or lard) and cabbage leaves, just as in the old technique for preserving meat, widespread in the Venetian countryside up until the beginning of the twentieth century, by alternating it with layers of lard and cabbage leaves. The feast of June 25 was called *San Marco dell'acqua rosata*, "St. Mark of the Rosewater," as on this day a priest went round the basilica with an altar boy, sprinkling first the high altar, then the clergy in the chancel and finally the congregation with rosewater, to commemorate the strong scent of roses that was given off when the saint indicated the place he was buried. The custom, recorded up until the middle of the nineteenth century, gradually fell out of use. On the same feast day the clergy used to cense the pillar where the saint appeared, i.e. the one on the right as you come out of the chapel of San Leonardo next to the crypt. The feast of October 8 was known as *San Marco delle zízole* ("St. Mark of the Jujubes"), as this was the time when the red berries were ripening in the hedges of Venetian gardens, in the lagoon and elsewhere. On April 25 the faithful used to come to venerate the so-called

16

General view of the interior of the basilica

The sequence of vaults and domes is the reflection of an essentially Byzantine scheme of construction that permitted the Greek architects, summoned to Venice by Doge Domenico Contarini in 1063, to adapt the requirements of the new building to the existing structures that the doge wished to preserve, such as the one that is now the crypt but was originally the place where the body of St. Mark the Evangelist was kept. The differences in size between the domes of the transept and the ones in the church's longitudinal axis and between the north and south ones in the transept itself are clear signs of the changes that were necessary to adapt the plan of the basilica to the existing situations to the north and south, as well as to incorporate the first church of St. Mark, now the crypt.

Finally, another significant factor in Venice was the need to distribute the weight of the church's walls, piers and domes over the largest area possible. The solution of repeating the same structural pattern many times was able to achieve the effect of grandeur that the Venetians so admired in the basilica of Hagia Sophia in Constantinople.

marble throne of St. Mark, now in the Treasury but previously kept in the basilica. The throne, on which the saint was believed to have once sat, came to Venice in 1451 from Grado, where it had been received as a gift – it is said – from the Byzantine emperor Heraclius around 630. In Venice it was regarded as a precious relic and capable of preserving or relieving anyone who sat on it from the pains of rheumatoid arthritis.

Some of the solemn rites celebrated in the basilica and recorded in the manuscript and printed ceremonials of St. Mark were honored by the attendance of the doge and his court. It should be remembered that the doge considered himself to be the vicar of Mark the Evangelist, with jurisdiction over the basilica and several other Venetian churches independently of the authority of the pope himself. He had almost the powers of a bishop, exercised where liturgical rights were concerned through the *canonicus primicerius*, his delegate in spiritual matters. In addition to his attendance of Mass, the doge played a part in various other phases of the celebrations, commencing with the procession in which he was accompanied from the Doge's Palace along the Scala d'oro and the Scala dei Giganti by staggered groups of his twelve dogal canons dressed in copes of gold lame, a parade of altar boys and the dogal court. The procession left the palace through the door called the Porta della Carta and entered the basilica through the Porta di San Clemente, continuing as far as the chapel of the same name. Here the doge entered the presbytery, where he was awaited by the primicerius and the papal nuncio. At this point the celebration of Mass commenced at the foot of the altar, in the manner depicted in the well-known eighteenth-century engraving by Visentini. The doge stood on the right, on the side of the lectern, in third place after the primicerius and nuncio. While these two climbed the altar to recite the *Introit*, he ascended his throne, set in the middle of the entrance of the iconostasis.

In the more solemn rites of Holy Week, the doge took daily part in the liturgical ceremonies, both in the morning and in the so-called *Matins of Darkness* in the evening, as well as in the Procession of the Palms on Holy Thursday and Good Friday and in the complicated ritual of the tomb on Holy Saturday. However, the doge was not present at the ceremony held on Holy Thursday evening when the relics of Christ's Passion, conserved then as now in the shrine next to the

Treasury, were displayed in St. Mark's. This concluded, as is documented in a picture painted by Gabriele Bella in the late eighteenth century, with a procession through the Piazzetta dei Leoni and St. Mark's Square itself, with insignia hung from the Scuole Grandi. On Good Friday morning the doge, dressed in mourning, attended the Mass of the Presanctified and the ritual of the adoration of the Cross, accompanied by the ambassadors, members of the signoria, magistrates and senators. And in the evening, after listening to the sermon on the Passion, he took part in the Procession of the Most Holy Sacrament through the basilica.

On the so-called patriarchal rite, still the subject of much debate and practiced in the basilica up until 1807 when the Roman one was imposed, a few comments taken from the most recent treatment of the question in the aforementioned work by Cattin (*Musica e liturgia a San Marco*, Venice 1990) will suffice. The patriarchal rite was not of Eastern origin, nor was it derived from the patriarchate of Aquileia, though this is where the name comes from. Rather it was a Roman rite common in the Latin Church, but with a number of unusual features, such as the use of the Roman psalm book, as in the Vatican basilica, while the rest of the Church followed the so-called Gallican Psalter, or of liturgical colors that differed from those of the Roman rite. A few of the basilica's liturgical chants survived even after 1807 but were finally dropped with the disappearance of Latin after the recent reforms. In essence they belonged to the current of Roman liturgy, embellished with virtuoso graces as in the chant of the *Epistle* and the *Gospel*, but producing a quite different effect in the chants of the *Lamentations* in Holy Week and in the readings at the first nocturn of the *Christmas Matins*. In these the velvety softness of the voices and their melasmas gave the impression, if not of remote origins in the Eastern Church or the synagogue, at least of a respectful antiquity.

17

Christ the Pantocrator Giving His Blessing, mosaic, replaced in 1506 by Maestro Pietro, bowl-shaped vault of the central apse

Christ the Pantocrator, in accordance with the instructions of the Procuratori De Supra, is represented with the same figures and inscriptions as the ancient Byzantine mosaic. A later restoration was carried out by Leopoldo dal Pozzo, in 1716.

THE ART OF ST. MARK'S

Ennio Concina

St. Mark's does not stand at the geographic center of the city: for symbolic reasons, medieval and Renaissance accounts locate this elsewhere. The site does not even coincide with the historical tradition of the *umbilicus urbis*, said to lie in the vicinity of San Luca or San Giacomo di Rialto. Nor is it a location dating from early times: the church's foundation had no connection with the miraculous appearances of Christ, the Virgin and the saints that induced St. Magnus, bishop of Venice, to choose the sites for the first churches erected in the city and around the lagoon. Up until the beginning of the nineteenth century, moreover, St. Mark's was not even the city's cathedral, a status that was assigned, throughout the Middle Ages and for most of the modern era, to the isolated church of San Pietro. And yet it stands at the center of Venice's historical and cultural space.

The original St. Mark's was created as a place of worship closely connected with the authority of the doge – reinforced by his role as the custodian of the evangelist's body. This was done quite deliberately by an ancient dynasty of tribunes that, through a whole series of architectural commissions in addition to the basilica itself, set out to present itself as a renewal of the grandeur of the past. In doing so, it pushed the existing works of architecture in the area, the churches of San Teodoro and Santi Geminiano e Mena, into the background.

Medieval sources and accounts seem to underline both a sense of continuity and a break with the past: when Doge Giustiniano Parteciaco laid down in his testament (829) that stones from Equilo and Torcello should be used for the new church, he was evidently not concerned solely with the salvage of materials, but wanted to incorporate significant remains from the past into the building.

Though it was erected alongside the church of San Teodoro – domed, richly decorated and linked with the memory of the Eastern empire to which the Venetic province had been subject – the new building did not use it as a model. As is specifically stated in the sources, it assumed a form of its own, an allusive one suited to the presence of the saint's mortal remains.

In fact, the first St. Mark's did not even have the basilican structure of the principal episcopal churches in Veneto, or even of the seat of the patriarch at Grado, the *Nova Aquileia*, though this too was connected with the memory of St. Mark: again the chronicles insist that it was based on the Holy Sepulcher in

18

The Holy Women, mosaic, 10th-11th century, museum of St. Mark's

The mosaic used to be set on the southwest pier of the dome of the Choir. Along with the weeping angel, still visible on the pier, they formed part of a picture of the *Deposition from the Cross* which was destroyed and covered with marble at the time of the construction of the present and third St. Mark's Basilica.

The dimensions of the figures, their position on the pier and their height above the level of the crypt suggest that they were part of the mosaic decoration of the second church, the one rebuilt in the years 976-78.

19

Saint Matthew and Saint Mark the Evangelists, mosaics, 11th-12th century, central portal of the atrium, left-hand niches of the entrance

These form part of the basilica's earliest mosaics which, owing to their position and the sturdiness of the walls to which they are attached, were less affected by the series of fires and earthquakes that struck the church in the first half of the 12th century.

20 *preceding pages*

Dome of the Ascension, mosaic, last quarter of 12th century, detail

Four angels in flight support Christ in the celestial spheres.

21-22

Agony in the Garden, mosaic, 13th century, south wall, dome of Pentecost

The work of three different mosaicists and executed sometime between 1214 and 1220, the panel is a faithful representation of the story of Christ praying in the Garden of Gethsemane, showing us the inability of the disciples to stay awake and the intense suffering of Christ himself. It depicts the natural setting, and in particular the flowers, vibrating against the gold ground as the tension builds up to a shattering event. It is one of the most intense, dramatic and moving of all the mosaics in the basilica.

Jerusalem. In other words, universal and sanctifying symbols were taken from the universal center of the world of devotion and transferred to the emerging power of Venice. Symbols which served to create an artistic center that was to a certain extent autonomous, and closely bound up with the authority of the doge, whose *pietas* and *auctoritas* the building was also intended to represent. Later it was to become the decisive location for the development of the image of the city-state, from the time of the medieval commune to that of the Renaissance republic.

After the renovation carried out by Pietro Orseolo, from 1063 onward, the dogal church was rebuilt and enlarged in a new architectural guise. The memory of the original *capella ducis* was reinterpreted and redefined in undisguisedly courtly terms, taking as its prototype – it is claimed – Justinian's church of the Holy Apostles in Constantinople. This church, a shrine for relics of the apostles and the imperial place of burial, was closely related to another church founded by Justinian, the basilica of St. John at Ephesus. On the one hand, then, the building housing the remains of Mark the Evangelist was given the same architectural form as the ones with the remains of Luke the Evangelist – venerated in the *Apostoleion*, or church of the Holy Apostles – and John the Evangelist, buried at Ephesus. On the other, the new construction clearly

symbolized Venice's imperial aspirations. From this time on, in fact, the great church in Venice was to breed, in a manner of speaking, a series of "lesser St. Mark's" in the Venetian quarters of the Levant and even Constantinople itself.

There is an extremely significant emphasis in the chronicles – probably of medieval origin and perhaps suggested by the bas-reliefs on the Arcone dei Mestieri of the central portal – on public participation in the construction: the nobility – it is said – contributed precious marble and money, while the common people pitched in with the labor of their hands. Thus St. Mark's was seen as a collective effort on the part of the *civitas* and commune, and not just as the chapel of the doge.

In the same way, the great cycles of mosaic, a Latin reinterpretation and translation of the decorations of Byzantium, and the complicated geometric patterns traced in *opus sectile* on the floor have led the collective imagination to

23-24

Dance of Salome, mosaic, 14th century, baptistery, lunette above the north door
Mosaic by the local workshop, dating from between 1343 and 1354. The mosaics in the baptistery, the work of two

different craftsmen, mark a phase of transition between the Byzantine Romanesque period and the fully Gothic one of Venetian culture. Elements of International Gothic can be discerned.

attribute their design to Joachim of Fiore and to see in them, inscribed for eternity, the mysteries of the destiny of humanity and the way toward its salvation.

From that time on St. Mark's became the repository for the signs and symbols of the rise of the *Comune Veneciarum* and its own sense of making history. The same feeling found expression in a long series of architectural interventions, sculptures and decorations in stone and mosaic that commenced in the early thirteenth century, during the time, that is, of the Eastern Latin Empire. The narthex was extended to both sides of the western arm of the church, the external and internal walls were faced with precious marble, bas-reliefs and two orders of columns that framed the deep-set portals, concealing from view the surface of the twelfth-century walls with their niches and decorative motifs in brick. The central portal and the *Porta da Mar* were fitted with bronze doors made in Constantinople during the reign of Justinian and above them were placed the four horses of the quadriga looted

25 *below*

Dormitio Virginis, mosaic, 15th century, Mascoli Chapel, southern side of the vault

In Tuscan Renaissance style, it can be compared with the one signed by Michele Giambono on the west wall, where the Venetian Gothic style is still evident in the architecture represented in the mosaic (see photograph on page 161). These are the earliest mosaics in the basilica for which a "cartoon" was used, a technique that seems to have been introduced by Paolo di Dono called Paolo Uccello, the Tuscan artist sent from Florence to Venice (1425-33) to reestablish the school of mosaic, which had recently died out.

26 *right*

Tree of Jesse, mosaic, 16th century, north transept, north wall

Also known as the *Family Tree of the Virgin*, who appears, with the Child, on the top of the tree that has Jesse at its root. The top is the place of Christ's union with humanity. The mosaic is the work of the mosaicist Vincenzo Bianchini to a design by Giuseppe Porta called Salviati (1542-52).

from the hippodrome of the Eastern capital. The sculptural group of the *Tetrarchs*, carved out of porphyry and taken from the square of the *Philadelphion*, was set up at the corner between the palace and the church. Two elegant pillars that may once have stood in the church of St. Polyeuctus in Byzantium were raised just a few paces away, so as to lend even greater magnificence to the southern ceremonial entrance to the basilica. Another addition to St. Mark's was the icon of the Virgin known as the *Nikopoia*: venerated as the sacred painting that had occupied a central place in the imperial liturgy, patron of the Romans and "leader of the legions," it had once been housed in a chapel of the imperial palaces.

So the structural and decorative renovation of the basilica should be seen as an assumption of *regalia insignia* on the part of the city. It certainly has to be interpreted as an artistic affirmation of the *translatio imperii*, of the conquest and surpassing of Byzantium, whose memory, sovereign magnificence and splendid emblems Venice now flaunted in triumph. Actually the symbolism extended even further: the slabs of rare polychrome stone – it is claimed – came from Aquileia and Ravenna as well as Byzantium, in other words from the three cities that epitomized both the history and the grandeur of the imperial idea as well as the origins of Venice.

The symbolic role of the art went even further. A group of columns in the narthex were claimed to be genuine relics of Solomon's temple, transferred from Jerusalem to Byzantium and from there to Venice, in testimony to the passage of the mantle of the *Nova Hierusalem* to the city of the Evangelist. Even the ritual of the uncovering of the *Pala d'oro* and the display of the church furnishings from the Treasury of St. Mark's on the high altar under the honorary roof of the baldachin appears to be a replica of the one conducted in Jerusalem, when David offered the booty from his victories to the temple of Solomon.

Changes were also made to the relationship between the church, the urban landscape and the square. The profile of the domes was altered, emphasized by the high extrados so as to impart an even greater visual impact to the sacred site of the city-state. The effect of the marble decorations and cycles of mosaics that herald the iconographic system of the interior from the outside is to transform the opaque screen of the front of St. Mark's into a luminous surface, a direct communication between the basilica's exterior and its sacred and liturgical recesses. Through the *Scenes of the Translation of Saint Mark's Body* the façade is turned into an unroofed ceremonial nave to the square, taking on the role of an immense and precious iconostasis.

From this moment on, through the Middle Ages and beyond, the art of St. Mark's would be seen as the heart of Venetian artistic culture. In the basilica "gleaming with Parian marble" Raffaello Zovenzoni would seek Antiquity, finding works equal to those of Scopas, Zeuxis and Polyclitus, which he knew from their literary descriptions. The art historians of the sixteenth century would see it as a yardstick and model of magnificence, and one that had already spread (San Giovanni in Oleo had a "structure [...] modeled on the middle part of the golden temple of St. Mark" and Santa Maria Formosa was "brought to perfection [...] on the model of the middle section of the church of St. Mark," wrote Francesco Sansovino). Its validity was to endure beyond the threshold of the Renaissance: according to Sansovino again, San Salvador, a renovation of great symbolic significance that was commenced in 1506, was "rebuilt [...] to a model [...] copied from the middle part of the church of St. Mark's." And by no coincidence, at the very center of the city which the new building served to reconsecrate.

27 *facing page at top*

The Descent of Christ into Limbo, mosaic, main façade, second lunette on the left
The work of the mosaicist Luigi Gaetano, to a cartoon by Maffeo da Verona. In 1617-18 the artist completed the entire upper level of the main façade, with the four lunettes illustrating the *Deposition from the Cross*, the *Descent into Limbo*, the *Resurrection* and finally the *Ascension of Christ*.

28 *facing page at bottom*

The Doge and the People of Venice Welcome the Body of Saint Mark, mosaic, 18th century, main façade, lower level, third arch on the right
This mosaic, which covers both the lunette and the vault of the arch, is the work of the mosaicist Leopoldo dal Pozzo, to a design by Sebastiano Ricci (c. 1730).

29 *following pages*

The Last Judgment, mosaic, bowl-shaped vault of the central portal, lower level
The mosaic is the work of the mosaicist Liborio Salandri, to cartoons by Lattanzio Querena (1836-38).

OVIS FRACTIS PORTIS, SPOLIAT ME CAMPIO FORTIS

TOUR OF THE BASILICA

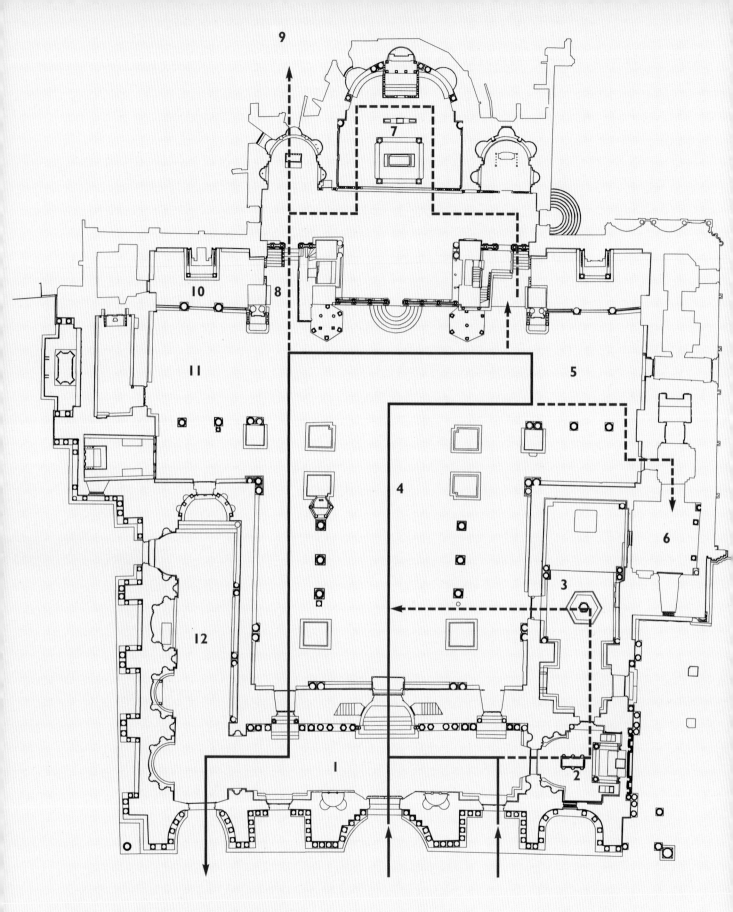

Legend

1. west atrium
2. Zen Chapel
3. baptistery
4. main nave
5. south transept
6. treasury
7. Pala d'oro
8. entrance to crypt
9. sacristy
10. Blessed Virgin Nikopoia
11. north transept
12. north atrium

THE TOUR OF THE BASILICA

Ettore Vio

We shall start our tour from the south front, the most enigmatic and extensively modified of the basilica's façades, and the one that appears in all views of the city. Then we shall move on to the west front, opening onto St. Mark's Square, where the key elements of the building's architecture are visible: the great arches that support the terrace, the lunettes of the structures above the basilica's atrium, the four bronze horses and the Gothic friezes with statues of saints, with that of Mark himself set in the middle. The façade is crowned by large domes faced with lead, an interpretation of a Byzantine model in a Western key that has no parallel elsewhere in the world.

In the north front, facing onto the Piazzetta dei Leoni, is set the Porta dei Fiori ("Door of the Flowers"). This leads into the atrium opposite the entrance to the north transept (used only by people going in to pray). We shall enter the basilica from the main façade.

The atrium or narthex, which was once entered from the south through the *porta da mar* ("sea door"), now turned into the Zen Chapel, is decorated with mosaics representing *Scenes from the Old Testament*. Passing through the Porta della Madonna ("Door of the Madonna") after the *Crossing of the Red Sea*, we come into the northern transept opposite the altar of the *Nikopoia*, or *Nicopeia* in the Latin transcription, an ancient icon brought to Venice as part of the booty from the Fourth Crusade.

The main entrance is through the portal with doors of "damascened" bronze, whose structure houses the oldest mosaics in the basilica. As you enter, you are immediately struck by the preciosity of the marble and mosaic facings and the proportions of an architecture that has no peer.

What you see is a succession of arches, vaults and domes, whose facing of golden mosaic catches the light entering through the windows in the dome, the large openings of the rose windows and the stained-glass window of the horses on the west façade, scattering reflections endlessly.

From the inside it is possible to appreciate the structural system that underpins the Greek-cross layout of the basilica's architecture. This consists of four piers united by four vaults with a dome on top, a pattern that is repeated five times.

The mosaics in the domes, lined up along the longitudinal axis, tell the *Story of Salvation* and indicate, in the dome of the prophets above the altar, the promise of a Savior. At the center of the crossing, the dome of the Ascension shows us the historical Christ and his witnesses, the four evangelists, in the pendentives that support it. The dome of Pentecost or the Holy Spirit, with the throne for the Christ that will come at the end of time (*Hetoimasia*), presents the apostles assembled at the Last Supper and filled with the Spirit of God.

The south transept, a part of the basilica used particularly often by the doge, is surmounted by the dome of St. Leonard, with Saints Nicholas, Blaise, Clement and Leonard (up until 1981 the altar dedicated to Leonard was used to house the Holy Sacrament). In the north transept, an area that pertained to the church's priests, headed by a *primicerius* whose residence was in what is now the patriarchal palace, we find the dome of St. John the Evangelist, epitome of priesthood, who strengthened the faith, overthrew idols and gave aid and succor to believers.

Our tour now takes us toward the crossing and allows us to appreciate the scale of the transept and to admire the iconostasis and the altar that houses the mortal remains of St. Mark, underneath a baldachin. Next we come, in the area to the left, to the ancient icon of the Blessed Virgin known as the *Nikopoia* and, on the right, to the altar of St. Leonard.

In the southwest corner is located the entrance to the Treasury. This is housed in a tower that used to be part of the doge's castle but which was later annexed to the basilica.

From here it is possible to visit the altar screen known as the *Pala d'oro* (for which a fee is charged) located behind the altar and then, by prior appointment, the sacristy with its mosaics dating from the early sixteenth century and inlaid work by the brothers Paolo and Antonio Mola, as well as the crypt, recently restored and reopened in 1993. From the atrium you can enter the Museo di San Marco: going out into the Corte Canonica, a staircase leads up to the museum, housed in the former banquet hall.

30

General plan of the basilica showing the internal and external routes

The description follows the route and, where the interior is concerned, moves from the right-hand side of the nave to the south transept, the presbytery and the two side chapels, the north transept and the left-hand wall of the nave on the way out. The exterior and the atrium or narthex are described separately.

THE EXTERIOR OF THE BASILICA

Ettore Vio

The basilica is not an easy building to grasp, owing to the substantial modifications and renovations of its magnificent image that were carried out over the first five centuries of its existence. The tour underlines the key points of the basilica's architecture and decoration.

We approach the building from the south, where it faces onto the first and ancient square of St. Mark, for 700 years the scenic backdrop to the "egresses" of the doge and the Signoria Serenissima in the direction of the wharf, the square or the church itself through the adjoining Porta della Carta of the Doge's Palace.

The southern front is characterized by pivotal elements of the basilica's architecture: the tower set at the corner between the Doge's Palace and the church that used to stand on the site before the construction of the first St. Mark's (829–32); and the *Porta da Mar*, the entrance used by navigators of all kinds from the twelfth century up until the beginning of the sixteenth,

31

Saint Mark with his Gospel at the top of the central pediment of the west façade

Set above the large stained-glass window called the "window of the horses," the image represents, in synthesis, the political authority expressed in the quadriga of St. Mark and the religious faith that took on a special accent in the Venetian veneration of the city's patron saint.

32

Exterior of the basilica, main façade

Here we see the basilica in all the harmony of its composition, in which every element tends to draw the observer's attention toward the central doorway. Above, the three domes of the nave emphasize the importance of the façade's median axis. Between the portal and the dome, the large window and the four horses further underline the significance of the main entrance. At the sides, the portals that create a visual link between the façade and the sequence of arches in the Procuratie Vecchie and Nuove.

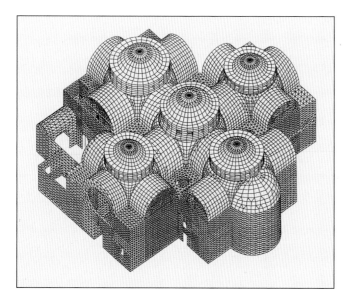

33

**Structural model of
St. Mark's Basilica, made by
the ISMES of Bergamo,
1992-93**

This model with all the basilica's
elements is used to assess the level
of stress on the wall structures.

34

View of the domes

The domes were built out of
wood and covered with lead – just
as we see them today – on top of
the Byzantine ones in brick.
The basilica's famous mosaics are
set on their inner surface.

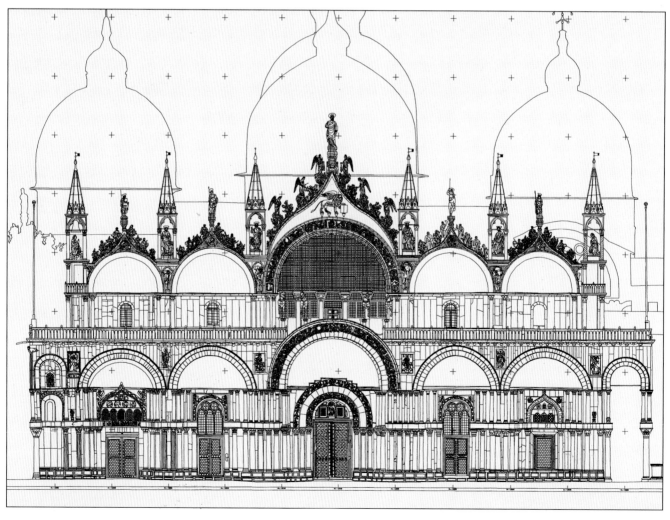

when it was walled up to house the tomb of Cardinal Zen. Between the two lies the baptistery, formerly the *giesia dei putti*, or "church of the putti," and initially a portico. At the beginning of the eleventh century this was frescoed with an *Ascension*, whose remains were uncovered during the restoration carried out in the 1960s. The present structure dates from the restoration of 1865-75 and the corrective interventions made in the years 1890-95.

The airy corner of the terrace supported by a double order of three columns, with a block of red granite called the *pietra del bando*, or "stone of proclamation," at their feet, leads to the west façade. The main front of the basilica has five large portals dating from the twelfth century, each with a lunette set in the level above. The central portal, adorned with three large arches carved in the lower level, is concluded above the terrace, behind the four horses, by a large window. This in turn is

35 *facing page at top*
W. Scott, after a drawing by A. Pellanda, Conjectural Original Design of St. Mark's Basilica, watercolor
The work shows the main façade in the state it was before the restoration work carried out in the second half of the 19th century. It is a hypothetical reconstruction of the appearance of the present basilica in the time of Doge Ordelaffo Falier (1094), before its brick walls were clad with marble.

36 *facing page at bottom*
Photogrammetric survey of the façade as we see it today, 1985-94

37
The Body of Saint Mark Arrives in Venice, mosaic, 17th century, main façade, lower level, second lunette and vault on the right
The mosaic was executed to a design by Pietro Vecchia (*c.* 1660).

surmounted by an arch, molded on the front as well as the inner surface. The statue of St. Mark is set at its apex.

This structure is laid over the original masonry of the eleventh century. The present and third basilica was clad with marble and adorned with columns in the thirteenth century. Gothic pediments were added by Tuscan stonecutters, active in the basilica in the first half of the fifteenth century. They also created the large "window of the horses" (1420–22) and the

38

Alberto Prosdocimi, Main Façade of the Basilica, watercolor, 1885-87
The artist painted this view of the façade and one of the interior of the church in preparation for the chromolithographs illustrating the great work on St. Mark's

published by Ferdinando Ongania: *La Basilica di San Marco in Venezia, illustrata nella storia e nell'arte da scrittori veneziani sotto la direzione di Camillo Boito, 1888-92.*

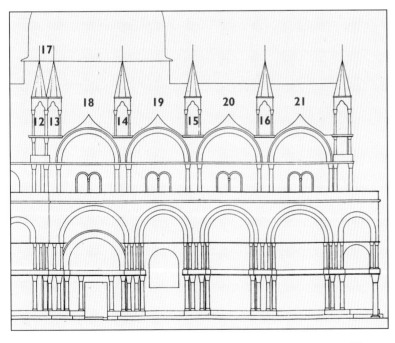

39-40-41

Schematic drawings showing the location of the sculptures

west façade

1. Archangel Gabriel
2. St. Matthew
3. St. Mark
4. St. John
5. St. Luke
6. Our Lady of the Annunciation
7. St. Constantine
8. St. Demetrius
9. St. Mark

10. St. George
11. St. Theodore

north façade

12. Archangel Michael
13. St. Gregory
14. St. Ambrose
15. St. Augustine
16. St. Jerome
17. Hope

18. Charity
19. Faith
20. Temperance
21. Prudence

south façade

22. St. Anthony Abbot
23. St. Paul the Hermit
24. Justice
25. Courage

Gothic rose window in the south transept facing onto the courtyard of the Doge's Palace.

The image of the west façade is completed by the domes covered with sheets of lead, erected in the thirteenth century above the Byzantine hemispherical vaults. The effects of the restoration carried out in 1855-65 are evident on the north façade, whose layout echoes the scheme of the western one: large expanses of the marble have been replaced. The Porta dei Fiori is located at the end of the narthex.

The mosaics make their first appearance in the vaults of the arches on the front facing onto St. Mark's Square, with the *Story of the Retrieval of Saint Mark's Body* from Alexandria. In fact the first scene on the right is the *Retrieval of Saint Mark's Body*, while the second represents the *Arrival in Venice*. Both mosaics date from the seventeenth century. The fourth is the *Homage Paid by the Signoria and the Doge to the Relics of the Saint*, an eighteenth-century work by Sebastiano Ricci and the mosaicist Leopoldo dal Pozzo. The fifth, which is the only surviving mosaic from the original thirteenth-century series, depicts the *Placing of the Saint's Body in the Basilica*. This constitutes the earliest view of the basilica with its marble facings and columns and the horses of St. Mark on the terrace. The sole record we have of the rest of the original mosaics is the large canvas by Gentile Bellini (1496), the *Procession with the Relic of the Holy Cross in the Square*, now in the Gallerie dell'Accademia. Bellini took the opportunity to present a basilica gleaming with gold and laden with sculptures after the intervention of the Tuscans and the repairs made following the devastating fires of 1419 and 1489.

On the upper level, the four lunettes, all the work of Maffeo da Verona (seventeenth century), illustrate the *Descent into Limbo*, *Resurrection*, *Deposition from the Cross* and *Glory of the Risen Christ*. The bowl-shaped vault over the central portal represents the *Last Judgment* with Christ and the Virgin Mother.

42 *preceding pages*

The Body of Saint Mark Leaving Alexandria, mosaic, 17th century, main façade, lower level, first lunette and vault on the right
The saint's body is placed in the basket with pork meat. The mosaic was executed to a cartoon by Pietro Vecchia (*c.* 1660).

43 *bottom*

Red porphyry head called the Carmagnola Head
Following the most recent comparative studies of images of Justinian, the head is now considered an image of the Byzantine emperor. The cut-off nose, which has also given the head its name of *rinotmetos*, may simply be the result of damage to the sculpture. The head is located in the southwest corner of the balustrade of the loggia above the narthex.

44 *facing page*

The Tetrarchs, sculpture in imperial red granite, 4th century
Set at the base of the corner tower of the Doge's Palace, the sculptural relief representing the four Tetrarchs, a product of Egyptian art, is placed as if it were the cornerstone of the palace to defend its chapel, the church of St. Mark, to which the tower was eventually annexed. It was also a symbol of the duchy's loyalty to the Byzantine empire and subsequently of the inheritance of its mantle and the continuity with its history. In popular tradition they are identified as four Moors, or Saracens, who attempted to rob the Treasury of St. Mark's.

45 *following pages top*

The Deposition of Christ from the Cross and the Descent into Limbo, mosaics, west façade, upper level, first and second lunettes to the left of the central arches
Both are the work of the mosaicist Luigi Gaetano (1617-18), to cartoons by Maffeo da Verona.

46 *following pages bottom*

The Resurrection of Christ and the Ascension, mosaics, west façade, upper level, first and second lunettes to the right of the central arches
Both are the work of the mosaicist Luigi Gaetano (1617-18), to cartoons by Maffeo da Verona. A remarkable feature is the presence of the lion of St. Mark on the flag held by the risen Christ, instead of the traditional red cross on a white field.

CRVCE DESCENDO SEPELIRI CVM NECE TENDO QVAE MEA SEPVLTA IAM SVRGAM MORTE RELICTA

CRIMINA QVI PVRGO TRIDVO DE MORTE RESVRGO ET MECVM IMVLTI DVDVM RECLVSE SEPVLTI

CAIETANVS · F · MDCXVII

EN VERVS FORTIS QVI FREGIT VINCVLA MORTIS ·

QVIS FRACTIS PORTIS, SPOLIAT ME CAMPIO FORTIS

THE GOTHIC DECORATION OF THE COPINGS

Guido Tigler

The mixtilinear profile of the basilica's façades is ringed at the top by a true crown of white marble, giving the solid block of the building an ethereal and fragile late Gothic summit. The vaults of the Byzantine type are inscribed in inflected arches (busts of saints are set in the resulting pendentives), decorated on the outside with carvings of large and serrated cabbage leaves stirred by the wind, alternating with busts of Prophets. On top of each arch stands the isolated statue of a saint venerated in Venice or the personification of a Virtue. Four of these figures (Constantine, Demetrius, George and Theodosius) were brought down by an earthquake in 1511 and replaced in 1618 with statues by Giorgio Albanese. The arch in the middle of the main façade is larger and has a taller external profile. In the intermediate space is set a lion of St. Mark against the background of a starry sky, a nineteenth-century cast-iron reproduction of the original one, destroyed in 1797. This more conspicuous cusp is surmounted by the statue of the evangelist to whom the church is dedicated, while six adoring angels with gilded wings are ranged along its sides. Between one arch and the next is set a tall Gothic aedicule (the one at the northwest corner, which also houses a bell, is dated 1384 and marks the beginning of work on this part of the basilica). Each of the aedicules (known as *capitelli* in the Venetian dialect) holds a statue. At the ends of the west façade stand the *Announcing Angel* and *Our Lady of the Annunciation*, repeating the arrangement of the slabs carved in relief on the lower part of the façade and alluding to the Venetian New Year and the mythical origin of the city on March 25, 421. The other four aedicules on the west façade contain the four *Evangelists*, while those on the northern side house the *Fathers of the Church* and on the southern one, two saints (*Anthony Abbot* and *Paul the Hermit*). Under the four central aedicules of the western side stand sturdy human figures holding leather water bags, squeezed into the restricted space of the niches set in the pendentives. These are the so-called spouts or "gargoyles" that must have once really served to collect the rainwater from the roofs behind while evoking the concept of the *Rivers of Paradise* (four more *Rivers*, though only two of them now survive, were located on the lower, thirteenth-century part of the west façade). The high reliefs of the arch around the central window, behind the horses, date from the same period: those underneath the arch represent the four *Patriarchs* of the Old Testament and the *Evangelists* beneath canopies, while the ones on the front depict episodes from the Old Testament inside hexagonal panels alternating with foliage. The greater part of the sculptural decoration – some of it carved from Carrara marble – must have been executed following the two recorded deliveries of marble from Lucca in 1414 and 1419. The documents also tell us the names of the artists who were probably in charge of the undertaking, Paolo di Jacobello dalle Masegne in 1414 and Niccolò di Pietro Lamberti from Florence in 1419. We do not know whether the work was affected by the fire that broke out on the roof in 1419. The statues in the aedicules were carved in the first, Venetian phase of the work, while that of St. Mark in the middle of the west façade and above all the reliefs of the central arch – full of references to Ghiberti and calling to mind the tomb of Doge Tommaso Mocenigo at San Zanipolo, i.e. San Giovanni e Paolo, executed by Niccolò di Pietro Lamberti and Giovanni di Martino from Fiesole in 1423 – date from the second and Tuscan phase. One of the Tuscan sculptors who worked on these figures was Nanni di

Bartolo, called Il Rosso, to whom three of the spouts on the north façade have been attributed (the gargoyles on the western side are closely related to the ones on Milan Cathedral, even though the attribution to the Milanese sculptor Matteo Raverti is without foundation). The hypothesis put forward by some that Jacopo della Quercia may have worked here cannot be confirmed.

47

Detail of the statue of St. Mark on top of the central pediment, main façade
The work of Niccolò di Pietro Lamberti (*c.* 1420), it includes a gilded stone lion, set at the saint's feet against the background of a blue mosaic with gold stars.

48

Detail of St. Mark the Evangelist inside a small Gothic bell tower, main façade
At his feet is set a gargoyle, the figure of a man pouring water from an amphora on his shoulders. The statues were carved by Tuscan stonecutters in the first half of the 15th century.

THE ARCHES OF THE CENTRAL PORTAL
Guido Tigler

The main entrance of the basilica is ennobled by a solemn and complex structure of niches, separated by precious columns. Its extrados rises above the level of the terrace, providing a visual base for the bronze horses. Thus in all likelihood this unusual "arch of triumph" was designed for that very purpose, to be crowned by the statues from Constantinople, just as it is evident that the mosaic on the vault has always been intended to serve as the iconographic fulcrum of the decoration. The present mosaic, dating from the nineteenth century, is but a pale shadow of the previous, seventeenth-century one, which in turn was a replacement for the original thirteenth-century mosaic. We have some idea of the appearance of the latter, which represented the *Glorious Second Coming of Christ before the Last Judgment* and the *Raising of the Dead*, thanks to an accurate view of St. Mark's in a picture painted by Gentile Bellini in 1496, now in the Accademia. So the subjects represented in the crowded reliefs of the three arches, two of which directly encircle the sixteenth-century tympanum while the third frames the upper vault, should be interpreted from an eschatological perspective. With this rich cycle of sculptures, embellished with gilding and polychromy of which extensive traces have recently been rediscovered (1982-87), the Venice of the thirteenth century – the age of "Scholasticism" – set out to provide itself with an element typical of the great Gothic cathedrals of Northern Europe: a portal whose iconographic program was at once didactic and, in places at least, agreeably worldly. On the underside of the first arch, the Devil and Lust, accompanied by Brutes, allude to the prevalence of evil in the world. The archivolt exemplifies the vices, set in that metaphorical "dark forest" which

represented life for the people of the Middle Ages, both through the allegory of hunting (on the left) and through the direct representation of ignoble acts (on the right). The intrados of the following arch depicts the twelve months of the year, represented as was customary in medieval art by their personifications, most of them engaged in agricultural activities. They are accompanied by explanatory scrolls and the appropriate signs of the Zodiac. The front, on the other hand, is decorated with female personifications of the Theological and Cardinal Virtues, the Beatitudes and Truth, some of them accompanied by attributes and scrolls with verses from the Bible. On the underside of the third arch, where higher relief has been used to compensate for the greater distance from the observer, we see the handicrafts of Venice (it is possible, though not supported by documentary evidence, that the "Crafts" correspond to the guilds who funded the work). Finally, the Prophets and a Sibyl are represented on the front of this arch. The concept that binds all these together is clear: while awaiting the return of Christ, humanity is offered a chance of spiritual progress by following a path that leads from sin to redemption through work and morality. In their choice of compositional and iconographic models, the arch of the Brutes, which is based on a type of archivolt common in the Venetian palaces of the thirteenth century, and that of the Virtues, whose prototypes are to be found in the late twelfth-century mosaics of the central dome of St. Mark's, derive from the local tradition (even some of the Crafts are based on mosaics in the basilica, this time the ones in the atrium dating from the 1220s). The lively little figures entwined by plant shoots on the front of the first arch, representing the Months and Crafts, are plainly derived from the Emilian

models of Benedetto Antelami and his followers. From a strictly stylistic point of view, however, all the sculptures on the portal, though varied, show signs of this "Western" influence, which is associated with the conventional name of the "Master of the Months of Ferrara," a sculptor who was active – in Venice as well – in the twenties of that century. The first two arches were carved in 1240 by Master Radovan at Traù (Trogir) in Dalmatia, while the third – in view of subsequent developments in the sculptural decoration of St. Mark's – has to be placed no later than the 1240s.

49
General view of the central portal
The center of the basilica is marked by the presence of four large, sculpted arches.
On the lower level, the first surrounds the entrance and is decorated with scenes representing the struggle between humanity and nature. The underside of the second (early 13th century) has the months of the year and the signs of the Zodiac, with an orderly sequence of activities connected with the seasons, while the front is adorned with Virtues and Beatitudes.
The third (mid 13th century), which concludes the lower level, illustrates the crafts on which the civil liberty of the people of Venice was founded, shown here supporting the Venetian community.
These three arches were restored between 1981 and 1987.
On the upper level, the fourth arch (first quarter of the 15th century) encloses the "window of the horses." On its underside we see the Evangelists and Prophets, while the front is decorated with *Scenes from the Old Testament*. The fourth arch was restored between 1987 and 1994.

THE HORSES OF ST. MARK

Licia Vlad Borrelli

For seven centuries, the resplendent team of four bronze horses has marked time on the façade of St. Mark's, overseeing so much of the history of the Repubblica Serenissima that they have become its proudest emblem. Yet their origins are far more remote. They came to the city among the rich spoils of war carried off by the Venetians, led by Doge Enrico Dandolo, after the conquest of Constantinople at the end of the Fourth Crusade (1204), along with other works of priceless value, many of them still conserved in the Treasury of the basilica today. The sack of the ancient capital of the empire is described in dramatic tones by the historians of the time, whether written from the viewpoint of the Crusaders or that of the Greeks, bearing witness to the massacres and other outrages that took place in the course of the amassing and sharing out of the precious booty. Yet none of them makes explicit mention of the horses. According to a disputed claim made by writers of the Renaissance era, they were dumped in the Arsenal for around fifty years, where they ran the risk of being melted down, until some Florentine ambassadors recognized their extraordinary quality and they were placed on the façade of the basilica. This probably occurred during the period of office of Doge Ranieri Zeno (1253-68) and formed part of the long and complex process of transformation and embellishment of St. Mark's linked to the growing wealth and power of the republic. The mosaic that decorates the lunette over the portal of St. Alypius, dating from around 1265, shows the horses already installed on the façade in the position they were to retain for centuries. A location that was to be celebrated by so many Venetian artists, commencing with Gentile Bellini's huge canvas of the solemn *Procession in St. Mark's Square* (1496), where the four

steeds appear in all their glory on the basilica's central loggia as if they stood on a great triumphal arch. An earlier, oblique reference to the horses of St. Mark, almost a citation, can perhaps be found in the scene of the *Expulsion of the Merchants from the Temple* in the Scrovegni Chapel, where Giotto sets two lions and two horses on the four pillars of the temple. Petrarch was the first to wonder about their origins. In a letter written in 1364 he extols their beauty and recognizes that they are ancient works, "whoever may have made them." However, it was only with the resurgence of interest in antiquity during the Renaissance that attempts were made to assign the horses a paternity, by attributing them to one of the great Greek sculptors: Ciriaco d'Ancona suggested Phidias, while others put forward the names of Praxiteles and Lysippus. This last attribution was to prove the most enduring, for a series of historical and archeological reasons. Lysippus was known, in fact, to have created a bronze four-horse chariot for the people of Rhodes and many scholars have attempted to identify this with the horses of St. Mark.

50

The four horses of St. Mark before restoration, in a photograph taken on the terrace

Note the difference in the surface of the horses before and after restoration. The originals have now been replaced by copies cast in bronze, their surfaces covered with an extremely thin layer of gold, applied with a wad, as they are considered an essential element of the façade's architecture and coloring.

The various theories have them taken first to Rome, or Persia, by one or another Roman emperor, and then transferred to Constantinople. The study of antiquity that developed in the late sixteenth and the seventeenth century discovered new references to the presence of quadrigae, or four-horse chariots, made of gilded bronze in the Byzantine sources. Confusing references were found to four horses "covered with gold" set above the starting positions in the hippodrome in Constantinople, brought there from Chios during the reign of Theodosius II, to a four-horse chariot with the sun god Helios set up by Constantine in the square known as the Milion and then transferred to the hippodrome, and to yet another team of four horses, also gilded and accompanied by a chariot and driver to which Constantine had had a statuette of Fortuna added to commemorate the foundation of the city in an annual ceremony. Which of these sculptures is to be identified with the horses on the façade of St. Mark's is still a moot point, though it is likely that they were located in the hippodrome, standing on four columns of porphyry that were mentioned by two

51

The horses of St. Mark, restored and placed in the museum above the narthex in 1982

The quadriga has been recomposed in the same order as the horses were arranged on the loggia, in two pairs with their heads turned toward each other. They have been placed at a height above the floor suitable for viewing from a distance of 8-10 meters.

European travelers in their description of the monuments of Constantinople written in the first half of the fifteenth century. A more attentive interpretation of the sources and various aspects of the group would have to wait, however, for the erudite climate of the eighteenth century, largely shaped by the founder of modern archeology, G. G. Winckelmann. The hypothesis was also put forward that they were not a Greek work at all, but one dating from the Roman era, and arguments over this attribution were to continue into the nineteenth century and right up to our own times.

One sad December in 1797, the four steeds were brought down from the façade of St. Mark's for the first time in over five centuries and, along with many other masterpieces, carried off to Paris by Napoleon. We know from contemporary prints and descriptions that the magnificent trophy of war was paraded through the streets of the city in a long procession, together with other booty brought back from Napoleon's successful campaigns. Given the role of decorating the triumphal arch of the Carrousel, they were harnessed to a chariot with two Victories and perhaps a statue of the emperor. The Parisian exile came to an end with the fall of Napoleon, when Antonio Canova was given the job of recovering the looted works and bringing them back to Italy. In a magnificent ceremony attended by Francis I of Austria, the new ruler of Venice, and staged on December 13, 1815, "after eighteen years, and on the very same day that they had been removed," the horses were put back in their places on the façade of St. Mark's. The precious team of gilded bronze horses, the only example to have survived from antiquity, had not come through these adventures unscathed. The horses had lost part of their collars, one head had been detached

and other damage had been inflicted, so that the horses had to spend a period in the Arsenal for restoration before being put back in their rightful place. Further interventions proved necessary over the following years, and the horses were brought down from their position above the main arch of St. Mark's on two more occasions, to be stored in a safe place during the last two world wars. As a consequence of these traumatic events, the natural deterioration of the material over the course of the centuries, the increase in airborne pollution and above all a more thorough understanding of problems linked with conservation, a series of technical examinations were carried out on the horses by the Istituto Centrale del Restauro in the sixties. These revealed that they were in a precarious condition, but also provided a great deal of valuable data on the history and morphology of the sculptures. The subsequent restoration was the first to be carried out on large bronzes with all the means that science is now able to place at the disposal of the arts. At the end of this long undertaking, it became apparent that in order to preserve the horses for the future it would be necessary to place them inside the museum of St. Mark and put up copies in their place above the arch, where for centuries they had stood as the proud emblem of Venice's power. An emblem that had led the Genoese conqueror of Chioggia, Pietro Doria, to exclaim to the three Venetian ambassadors who came to sue for peace in 1379: "Venetians, we shall never make peace with you until we have placed halters on those unbridled horses set on top of the temple of the divine Mark." It was a difficult and disputed decision, but the thin layer of gold that covered the bronze was lifting off in a number of places and pocked with tiny craters, cracks and scratches, harboring the

products of a long and irreversible process of corrosion, driven by the salts and acids present in the Venetian atmosphere. The scientific analyses permitted an all-round examination of the sculptures. They had been cast in several pieces (head, trunk, legs and tail) by the most indirect method, i.e. with concave blocks carved out of a mould. These were then covered with a layer of wax that was melted and replaced by molten metal: a particularly difficult operation in this case, as is evident from hundreds of different-shaped plugs used to fill the casting defects. In fact the alloy was made up almost exclusively of copper and had a much higher melting point than the usual form of bronze: a very rare, if not unique example of such a material being used for statues of these dimensions, but one that was done with the application of a layer of gold in mind. This proves that the gilding was intended right from the start, and was not applied subsequently, during the Roman era, as some had supposed. The gilding was probably carried out by two processes, using both gold leaf and gold powder mixed with mercury. The latter technique was in particularly wide use in the middle of the imperial Roman era. The artist toned down the glitter of the gold by engraving the areas most exposed to the light with dense hatching: this explains the existence of a series of scratches that had aroused a great deal of curiosity in the past, but which electronic analysis now shows unequivocally to have been deliberate. Roman numerals are carved on the hooves and halters. These have been attributed to measurements of weight, but their real function has never been clarified. The detailed analysis carried out during the most recent restoration has not brought any objective facts to light that would permit us to assign them a definite date, something which is made particularly difficult by the unique character of these

52

Restored head of a horse
The large expanse of gilded surface brought to light by the restoration is clearly apparent. The artist who originally carried out the gilding used scratching to prevent reflections from the surface masking the modeling of the sculpture. The scratches were only applied to parts exposed to sunlight.

sculptures. Doubts remain and the date of birth assigned to them by scholars – and there is no parallel to this in the history of ancient art – ranges from the fourth century BC to the fourth century AD. Yet there are a few clues, such as the use of mercury in the fusion, the form of the eyes, mane and ears and the complicated shape of the plugs used to repair casting defects prior to gilding, and therefore at the time of their execution, which suggest that the statues date from the Roman era, around the time of Septimius Severus, and were produced by a school of Greek-Oriental artists who had kept alive the great Hellenistic tradition. It is to be hoped that advances in the science of conservation will one day allow them to be put back on the front of the basilica, where Goethe saw them and was entranced by their powerful grace: "from close-up they look heavy, but viewed from below, from the square, they seem as slender and lithe as deer."

THE NARTHEX

Ettore Vio

The atrium or narthex plays a decisive part in the architecture of the north and west façades. The outer wall of the narthex was set against the large arches that support the terrace of the horses, which offers a wonderful view of St. Mark's Square, the Piazzetta and wharf and the lagoon with its islands. The structures that house the museum of St. Mark rest on these arches.

The narthex contains the graves of a number of illustrious doges who made a contribution to the basilica: on the right as you enter, Ordelaffo Falier († *c.*1086-96), who consecrated the church in 1094; on the left as you enter, Felicita Michiel († 1101), the wife of Doge Vitale Michiel († *c.*1096-1104) who, though engaged in continuous battles far away from Venice, dedicated much energy and effort to the completion of the basilica through his wife.

Other doges present are Marino Morosini († 1253) and Bartolomeo Gradenigo († 1342), in the north atrium; opposite the Porta dei Fiori stands the tomb of the *primicerius* Recovrati († 1420), who was certainly connected with the great undertaking of modifying the outer parts of the façade in the Gothic style.

There are two more significant elements of the narthex: the *Porta da Mar*, walled up in 1501-15 to house the tomb of Cardinal Zen, and the great bronze doors of the outer portal, which have recently been dated to the end of the tenth century.

Starting at the *Porta da Mar*, the domes, vaults and arches of the atrium depict scenes from the Old Testament.

In the bowl-shaped vault St. Mark is represented in ecstasy and dressed in bishop's robes: executed by the Zuccato brothers, its cartoon is attributed to Lorenzo Lotto (1545). Likewise, the episodes of the *Passion and Death of Jesus Christ*, on the wall of the "well," are considered to be some of the finest mosaics of the sixteenth century. A substantial part of the magnificent vault of the Apocalypse can be viewed through this opening.

The bronze doors (nineteenth century) on each side of the portal lead to the museum above and to the terrace.

All the external gates have two leaves, each cast in a single piece with panels and arches, on the model of the first portal (that of St. Peter) to the left of the central one, dated and signed "MCCC - Magister Bertucius Aurifex Venetus me fecit." Only the middle portal is closed by wooden doors faced

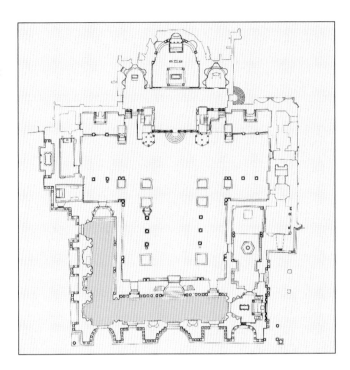

53 *opposite*

View of the western atrium

The sequence of mosaics with scenes from the *Old Testament*, based on the iconography of the *Cotton Bible*, forms a splendid adornment to this place separate from the basilica, as is apparent from the numerous columns supporting vaults and domes that are not part of the church's structure.

54 *above*

Plan of the basilica showing the area of the narthex

The origin of the narthex has been the subject of studies and hypotheses that have not always reached the same conclusions. It is certain that its structure is separate from that of the basilica: this is clear from the columns set against the walls of the church as both decoration and supports for its arches, vaults and domes. The slightly pointed shape of the arches in the north arm is reminiscent of the Byzantine architecture of the 7th-10th century and this has led some scholars to postulate that the first church was preceded by a cloister. It is not impossible that the present structure of the atrium derives from the transformation of an ancient portico, set against the boundary wall of the ducal *castrum-castellum*.

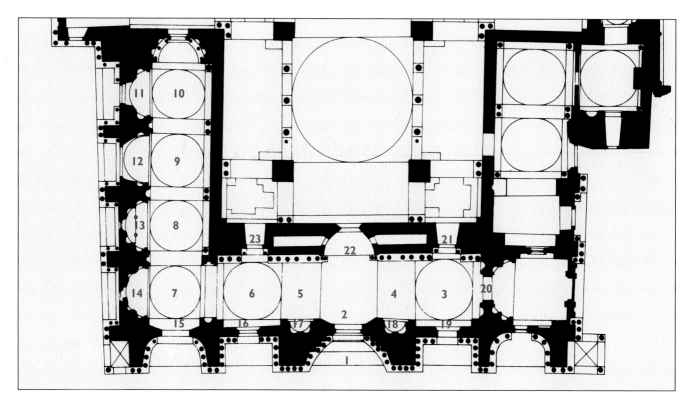

55

Plan of the narthex showing the location of the parts and the principal decorations

The mosaics represent in sequence: *Genesis* (1st dome), *The Flood* (1st vault), *Scenes from the Story of Noah* and the *Tower of Babel* (2nd vault), *Scenes from the Story of Abraham* (2nd dome), *Scenes from the Story of Joseph* (3rd, 4th and 5th dome), *Scenes from the Story of Moses* and the *Crossing of the Red Sea*, after which we enter the north transept through the door surmounted by the *Virgin Enthroned with the Infant Jesus*. The mosaics are the work of a local workshop, active between 1220 and 1285 according to Otto Demus. Opposite the main entrance, the architecture of the narthex is interrupted by an opening in the roof, called the "well." This may have been created to preserve the integrity of the apsidal vault of the central portal, whose doors of damascened bronze decorated with figures of Saints are inlaid with silver foil: a Byzantine work from the first half of the 12th century, they are flanked by some of the oldest mosaics in the basilica (11th and 12th century) representing the *Four Evangelists*, above the *Virgin between the Apostles*.

In addition to the works mentioned, it is worth drawing attention to the Renaissance design of the floor, by Paolo Uccello, in front of the Porta di San Pietro, and the large slab of red Verona marble that commemorates, at the entrance, the meeting between Pope Alexander III and Frederick Barbarossa to sign a peace treaty on July 23, 1177.

1. central portal
2. wooden door faced with bronze (10th century)
3. cupola of Genesis
4. The Ark and the Flood
5. Death of Noah and the Tower of Babel
6. cupola of Abraham
7. first cupola of Joseph
8. second cupola of Joseph
9. third cupola of Joseph
10. cupola of Moses
11. Porta dei Fiori
12. tomb of Primicerius Recovrati
13. tomb of Doge Marino Morosini
14. tomb of Doge Giovanni Gradenigo
15. gate of St. Alypius
16. gate of St. Peter
17. tomb of Felicita Michiel
18. tomb of Doge Falier
19. gate of St. Clement
20. gate of the Zen Chapel
21. Porta di San Clemente
22. central door
23. Porta di San Pietro

56

Dome of Genesis, first on the right in the atrium

The *Story of Creation* is narrated in twenty-five scenes, all with inscriptions, and the sequence of days is identified by the number of angels present, from one on the first day to seven on the last. Mosaic executed by the early local workshop, first half of 13th century.

with bronze, to which two large gratings (seventh century) are attached, along with ten stylized lions, nine of them of Persian origin (tenth-eleventh century) and one Venetian (twelfth-thirteenth century).

The doors between the atrium and church are faced with sheets of bronze. In the north arm we find the nineteenth-century Porta della Madonna. In the west one, on the other hand, there is the Porta di San Pietro on the left, with its twelfth-century Byzantine panels set in a sturdy frame, and the Porta di San Clemente on the right: probably the middle door in the second church (976-78), this is made of damascened bronze like the central one (late eleventh century). Finally, there is the large gate with small arches, made out of gratings (seventh century) identical to the ones fixed on the outside of the central doorway.

The floor of the atrium presents a great variety of designs, as does that of the interior.

57

Creation of the Fish and the Birds, mosaic, 13th century, atrium, dome of Genesis

Mosaic executed by the early local workshop, dating from the first half of the 13th century.

58

The Creation of Eve, mosaic, 13th century, atrium, dome of Genesis

Mosaic executed by the early local workshop, dating from the first half of the 13th century.

…ILITVDINE·NRÃ·ETBÑDIXDIEI

…RE·ÞDÑS·ICPÞ·DA·IPE·MOFTÃ·VXORE·F…

59 *preceding pages*

God Blessing the Seventh Day, mosaic, 13th century, atrium, dome of Genesis

Mosaic executed by the early local workshop, dating from the first half of the 13th century.

60 *above*

The "Go Forth and Multiply" mosaic, 13th century, atrium, dome of Genesis, east lunette

This mosaic, by the early local workshop, is set above the Porta di San Clemente.

61 *below*

Scenes from the Story of Noah, Emergence from the Ark, mosaic, 13th century, western atrium

The image is completed and enclosed by a rainbow, a mark of the new pact of alliance between God and humanity.

62 *facing page*

St. Mark in Bishop's Robes, atrium, semidome of the central portal

Mosaic by Francesco and Valerio Zuccato, to a cartoon by Titian or Lorenzo Lotto (1545).

THE MOSAICS

Maria Da Villa Urbani

When Venice decided to renovate the structure that housed the precious relics of St. Mark, patron and protector of the city, the plan was to create a *magna giesia*, a great church that would bear witness to the expansion of both the city and the state under the rule of Doge Domenico Contarini (1043-71), as well as to the growing economic, civil and political importance of the Serenissima. As we know, the model was found in Constantinople, in the church dating from the reign of Emperor Justinian (sixth century) and dedicated to the Twelve Apostles. This choice found its justification in the fact that– especially in the East – the evangelists Mark and Luke were traditionally included among the twelve.

Five domes, one in each arm and one set above the central space of the crossing, supported by vaults that stand on angular piers with four feet, make up the magnificent Greek-cross structure, which was designed from the start to be covered with mosaics on the upper part of the walls. While there were earlier precedents for such a decoration in Italy (in Rome and the basilicas of Ravenna), St. Mark's Basilica has to be considered of Byzantine derivation, owing to the evident reference to a precise figurative typology and to the documented presence of "Greek" mosaicists, i.e. from the Byzantine empire, who must have taught the art to the Venetians.

The mosaic decoration of St. Mark's, as we see it today, is a fascinating palimpsest, the product of a complex process covering the entire history of this church and lasting for some eight centuries. The original nucleus, executed over the course of the twelfth century, follows the iconographic program drawn up by a Venetian theologian who took the basic lines from the Byzantine tradition but freely reinterpreted them. The

mosaics set out to convey the great message of Christian salvation, centering on the three domes in the nave, those of the Prophets, the Ascension and Pentecost, masterpieces by anonymous artists who, under the "skin" of gold tesserae, a traditional symbol of Heaven, created three precious symphonies of color representing prophets and apostles according to the canons of Eastern iconography. Around these are set lesser groups of mosaics with special ties to Venetian piety: the *Scenes from the Life of Saint Mark* in the choirs at the sides of the main altar, the *Scenes from the Life of the Virgin* in the two transepts and the numerous figures of saints in the other two domes and the small vaults.

The decoration of the atrium was carried out over the course of the thirteenth century. In the extensive and varied group of mosaics modeled on early Christian miniatures and depicting scenes from the first five books of the Old Testament, it is possible to trace the evolution and

63 *right*

Dome with Scenes from the Story of Abraham, mosaic, 13th century
Like the other mosaics in the atrium, this dome, the second on the right, has inscriptions explaining the scenes represented. The inscriptions are blended into the decoration to form a single design. Mosaic executed by the early local workshop, dating from the middle of the 13th century.

64 *below*

Dome with Scenes from the Story of Abraham, detail of the inscriptions of a scene, mosaic, 13th century
Mosaic executed by the early local workshop, dating from the first half of the 13th century.

maturation of the language and style used by the mosaicists, who were now entirely Venetian: the figures no longer stand out in isolation against the gold ground, but are placed in natural or architectural settings of ever increasing complexity. Beautiful thirteenth-century mosaics can also be seen inside the church itself (the tablets – pinakes – with prophets on the walls of the nave and the two large panels representing the Agony in the Garden and the Finding of the Body of St. Mark), as well as on the ceiling of the Zen Chapel, where they depict Scenes from the Life of Saint Mark, and the bowl-shaped vault of the portal of St. Alypius, on the façade, which represents the Formal Entry of the Saint's Body into His Basilica. This last is the only thirteenth-century mosaic to have survived on the outside of the building. The two major cycles of mosaics in the baptistery and the chapel of St. Isidore were commissioned by Andrea Dandolo (doge from 1343 to 1354): here we find stylistic innovations of Western derivation, filtered through the work of Paolo Veneziano, the great founder of the Venetian school of painting, grafted onto the Byzantine tradition.

The mosaic decoration of the "new" chapel of the Madonna, later known as the Mascoli Chapel after the confraternity that used to meet in prayer there from 1618 onward, dates from around the middle of the fifteenth century. The mosaics in this chapel, which present five scenes based on episodes from the life of the Virgin drawn from the canonical and apocryphal Gospels, are an interesting testimony to the evolution of artistic taste in the Renaissance sense during this period. The final contribution, dating from the early part of the sixteenth century, is the precious and absolutely original ceiling of the sacristy, which had been renovated to a design by Giorgio Spavento, the proto, or

curator of the fabric of St. Mark's, between 1486 and 1493. We have documentary evidence for the involvement of Titian and his workshop in the design of the figures of prophets and apostles that encircle the great central cross, set against a tapestry of plant ornamentation in accordance with the canons of the High Renaissance.

It should be pointed out here that while the conception and execution of a mosaic had formerly been the work of a single person, who designed the figures on the basis of fixed models, drew the sinopia on the mortar that would form the support and then laid on the enamel tesserae, a division of the tasks had been introduced at some unspecified time, perhaps the beginning of the Quattrocento. From that time on a painter was entrusted with the task of producing a cartoon and then this was translated into mosaic by a skilled craftsman, using the technique of pouncing. From the sixteenth century onward, all the great painters of the Venetian school (Titian, Tintoretto, Veronese, Jacopo Palma il Giovane) worked on mosaics for St. Mark's. It has also to be said that, after the cycle in the sacristy and the family tree of the Virgin in the north transept, the many works executed over the course of the sixteenth, seventeenth and eighteenth centuries were all replacements for existing mosaics. In fact mosaics that crumbled away or were permanently ruined by fires, earthquakes or other violent events could be remade, so long as certain precise and well-documented indications were followed, at the behest of the procuratori di San Marco de supra, or high procurators of St. Mark, the State magistracy responsible for administration of the church. Although it was permissible to use a new and modern style, the mosaics had to represent the same scenes as before, so that they would fit into the original iconographic program, and the

same words had to be repeated in the inscriptions. The chosen painter was obliged to depict "the same scene and letters, that are there at present, without altering anything at all."

A clear example of this is provided by the vault located between the ancient domes of the Prophets and the Ascension (twelfth century), which have remained essentially intact in spite of many restorations: the original scenes recounting the beginning of Jesus's historical life (the Annunciation, Adoration of the Magi, Presentation in the Temple, Baptism and Transfiguration) were replaced between 1588 and 1589 by the same scenes to designs by Jacopo Tintoretto, who brought to the mosaics, executed by Giannantonio Marini, the rich coloring and inventiveness of the painter's many canvases of similar subjects.

65

Axonometric views of the three levels of mosaics in the basilica viewed from below and the southwest

The three drawings show the different levels of the mosaics in the basilica: the ones on the underside of the lower arches (top left), the vaults (above) and the domes (opposite).

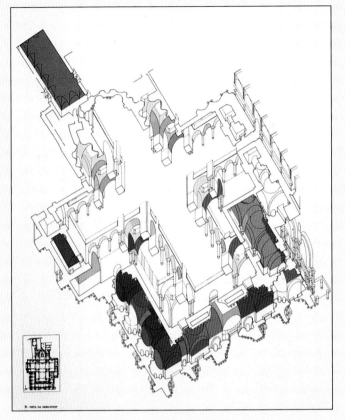

Legend

The colors identify the age of the mosaics. Each century, from the 11th to the 19th, is represented by a substantial proportion of the mosaic decoration on the inside and outside of the basilica. The shades, from the lightest to the darkest, indicate the period at which the mosaics were executed, starting with the oldest.

Gray	11th century
Light yellow	1st half of 12th century
Dark yellow	2nd half of 12th century
Orange	1st half of 13th century
Red	2nd half of 13th century
Dark green	14th century
Light green	15th century
Light blue	16th century
Dark blue	17th century
Brown	18th century
Purple	19th century

THE PORTA DA MAR

Ettore Vio

Since ancient times, it had been the custom for a sailing people to arrive at their destination by water, leaving the boat, whether large or small, at the foot of a grassy bank or a landing adorned with stone steps. The ancient ducal *castrum-castellum*, now the Doge's Palace, was surrounded by the waters of the lagoon and a broad canal: a harbor-cum-canal on the western side, in the direction of the basilica's south façade. Thus it was easy for the Venetians to enter the church from the southern end of the atrium, through the door that had always been known as the *Porta da Mar* ("sea door"): it was used by humble fishermen, sailors and great naval commanders up until 1501. It was then walled up to be turned into the chapel of Cardinal Zen, an omen of the end of Venice's dominance of the sea and trade with the emergence of new routes to the

West following the discovery of America by Columbus in 1492. But the decline may have had a deeper cause, a waning of ambition and drive in the Venetian society of the day.

Originally an apsidal portal crowned by early Romanesque statues, it was enlarged by the addition of a deep tunnel vault. This was intended to serve as a support for the terrace at the time of the renovation of the façade. Two lions with columns on their backs were carved to support the structure, but were never used owing to modifications made to the architecture. We have no pictures of the *Porta da Mar*. Even the perspective view by Jacopo de Barbari, dated MD (1500), where the south front of the basilica is visible in the foreground, shows the large doorway already walled up, though this was not actually done until 1501. However, the

lintel of the portal with statues representing the *Annunciation* can still be seen in the Treasury of St. Mark's.

66 *bottom*
Niche of the former Porta da Mar, apsidal semidome

The Virgin and Child are located at the center while the Archangels paying homage to them are at the sides. The mosaic of the Madonna was renovated in the second half of the 19th century, with extensive restoration of the two Archangels.

67 *right*
View of the former Porta da Mar from the south

When arriving by water, the Venetians used to disembark in the vicinity of the Doge's Palace and then go to pay their respects to St. Mark. The door was later closed and converted into the Zen Chapel.

THE INTERIOR OF THE BASILICA

Ettore Vio

The impression that the basilica makes on anyone entering it for the first time is a profound one. The light glinting on the mosaics and the succession of arches, vaults and domes, forming a vista that draws the eye toward the main altar, requires a period of contemplation so that the visitor can adjust to this almost unreal setting, made up of a blend of light and shade, of scintillating mosaics and precious marble. The first time you go into St. Mark's it is a good idea not to concentrate too much on the details but to let yourself be carried away by the atmosphere. St. Mark's is worth many a visit.

The basilica has a regular plan in the form of a Greek cross, with an elongated stem. The nave ends in a presbytery, which is raised by around sixty centimeters. The interior is roofed by five large domes resting on a system of round-headed vaults supported by enormous piers. Four of the domes are set above the arms of the cross, while the fifth is at the center. In fact the structural system of the basilica is based on the set of members that supports each dome and which is repeated, with adjustments made to the surrounding situation, five times. The same system can be found on a smaller scale in the structure of the piers: each one is made up of four pillars linked together by vaults at two levels and topped by a cupola.

The eleventh-century church was not clad with marble and the Byzantine moldings that mark the beginning of the vaults and domes formed the lower limit of the basilica's first mosaic decoration. The rest was built out of unplastered brick on the inside as well as the outside, frugally adorned with columns, capitals, plutei and bas-reliefs set in the walls. It was only under Doge Vitale Michiel II (1156-72) that the work of installing the marble facings commenced. Subsequently mosaics were set in the space between the Byzantine moldings and the marble. Each arm of the cross is divided into a nave and two aisles, with the two aisles about half as wide as the nave.

The columns and capitals are one of the great glories of the architecture and decoration of St. Mark's. There are numerous Byzantine capitals, dating from between the sixth and eleventh century, in the shape of baskets or truncated pyramids, covered with floral motifs and decorated with figures of animals. Note the six gilded capitals with ram's heads in the nave and the ten with acanthus leaves set on the pillars of the transept.

The floor is in *opus sectile* and *opus tessellatum*. It is a twelfth-century work that has been recomposed many times, adjusted and added to, with geometric designs and decorations with figures of animals. The floor, according to recent studies by Polacco, presents an abstract version of the iconographic themes in the mosaics above. Below the central dome of the Ascension, for example, the floor is made up of a large central panel of marble from Proconnesus, made up of twelve slabs of 1·5 by 4·5 meters each, forming a single block. They are a representation of Christ as the *lapis angularis*, the cornerstone of his Church, the element that provides support through the twelve apostles and their successors.

Two levels can be distinguished in the church: the upper one of the mosaics, above the marble facing, and the lower one. From the crossing we can see the majestic iconostasis that separates the presbytery from the nave. It is an unashamedly precious piece of work from the late fourteenth century, a screen made up of columns of fine oriental marble and plutei made out of large slabs of equally precious marble.

The presbytery, the basilica's sacred space, contains the high altar, under which is set the marble sarcophagus containing the mortal remains of St. Mark. Jacopo Sansovino, *proto* and architect of St. Mark's from 1529 to 1570, was responsible for important works of decoration.

The high altar is enclosed by a baldachin consisting of a groin vault encrusted with verd antique marble and supported by four alabaster columns decorated with scenes.

The layout of the presbytery, apart from recent alterations made following the transfer of the basilica to the patriarch of

68

Interior of the basilica

Here we can see the sequence of domes and vaults that characterize the nave and two aisles. Originally galleries were set above the columns that separate the nave from the aisles and used by women to attend services. As long ago as the 12th century, however, following the fire of 1145, many of the women's galleries were eliminated and reduced to the walkway we see today. In the 13th century, after further fires, the rest of them were demolished as well.

Their floors were made of wood and the part of the wall to which they were fixed is still clearly visible, as it was covered with slabs of red Verona marble, decorated with small sculptures. The parapets that line the walkway differ greatly in style and age. The ones facing onto the nave were made out of plutei dating from between the 6th and the 11th century, while the ones facing onto the aisles, constructed after the elimination of the women's galleries, consist of small marble columns with no decoration.

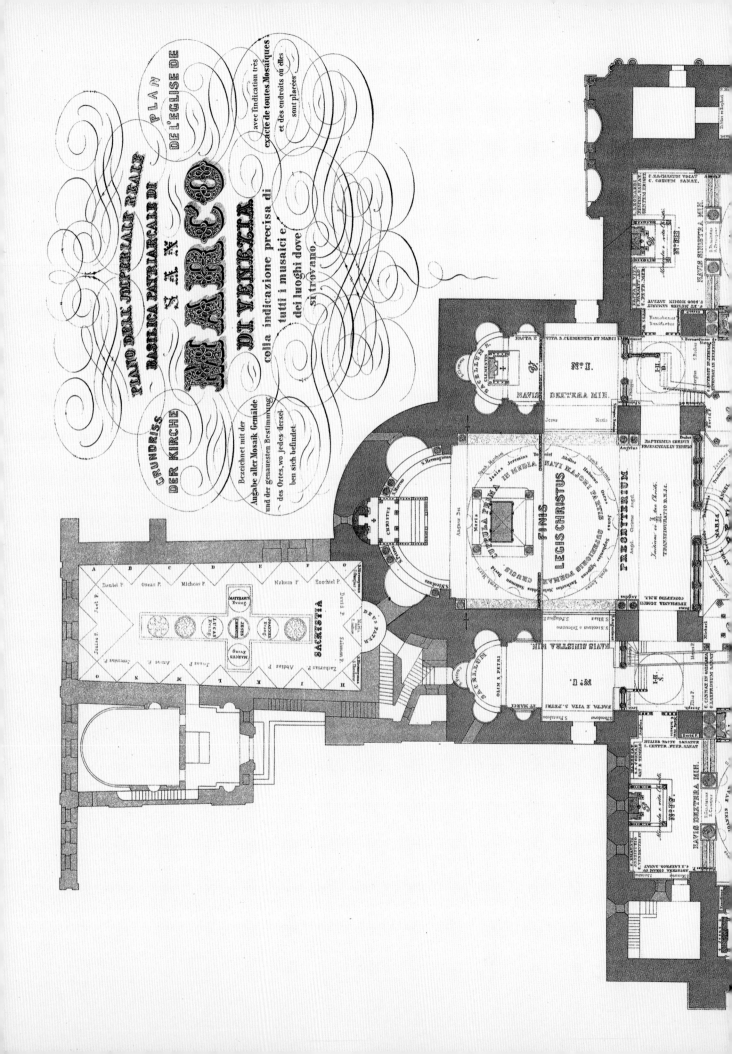

PLAN
DE L'EGLISE DE
GRUNDRISS
DER KIRCHE
PIANO DELL'IMPERIALE REALE
BASILICA PATRIARCALE DI
S A N
MARCO
DI VENEZIA

avec l'indication très
exacte de toutes Mosaïques
et des endroits où elles
sont placées

colla indicazione precisa di
tutti i musaici e
dei luoghi dove
si trovano

Bezeichnet mit der
Angabe aller Mosaik Gemälde
und der genauesten Bestimmung
des Ortes, wo jedes dersel-
ben sich befindet

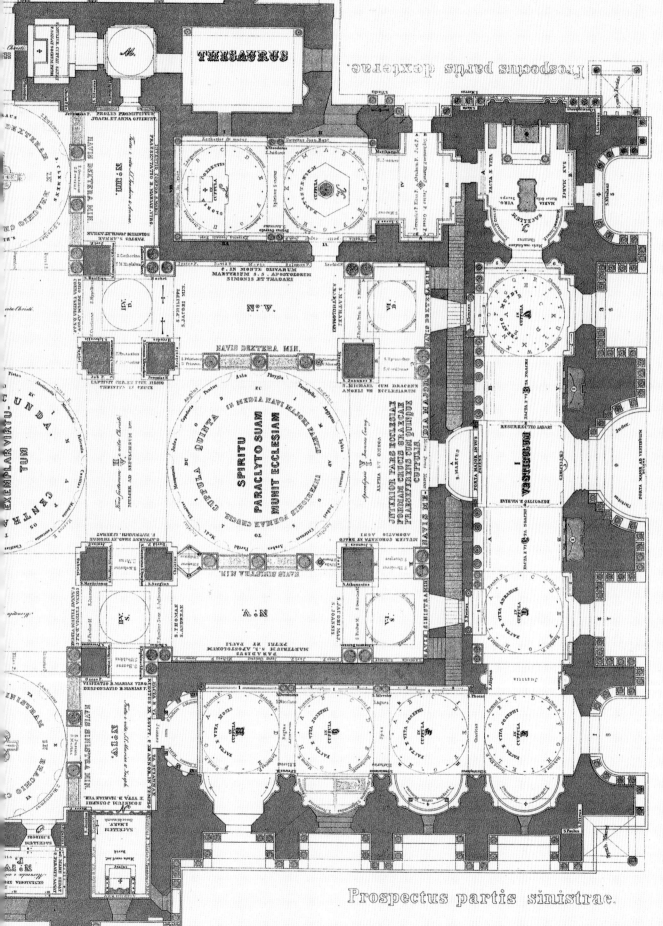

FACIES ECCLESIAE.

della litografia di Rath.

Prospectus partis dexterae.

litogr. F. Weiss.

Prospectus partis sinistrae.

Diseg. e dispos. da Giov. e Luig. +

69 *preceding pages*

G. and L. Kreutz, Plan of St. Mark's Basilica, lithograph by F. Weifs, Vienna 1843

The drawing represents the "Plan of the Imperial Royal Patriarchal Basilica of St. Mark in Venice" and shows where the various mosaic panels are located in the basilica, differentiating them on the basis of a careful analysis of the type of lettering used in the inscriptions, as well as their importance and height.

The entire surface of the walls above the marble facing is decorated with mosaics, covering a total of about 8600 square meters. An embellishment that has grown steadily over the centuries and that has earned the monument its nickname of the "Golden Basilica."

The mosaics are the living compendium of an art handed down by the republic of Venice through its mosaicists, ensuring respect of an iconography that has been assigned a political and social value in addition to a religious one.

Many of the mosaics on the domes, the pendentives and the vaults that support them are of Byzantine origin. They were restored and added to during the Renaissance, replaced where they were threatening to come away in the sixteenth to seventeenth centuries and underwent modest additions in the 18th century. Finally they were subjected to extensive restorations from the 19th century to the present day.

The iconography

The iconography, based on a Greek model, emphasizes the particular functions assigned to the different parts of the church as well as the presence, role and duties of the doge, who occupied the right-hand side of the building, and of the primicerius, who carried out his activities on the left-hand side.

In addition to corresponding to the functions and significance of different parts of the basilica, the mosaics are subdivided vertically. Starting from the top, the godhead is represented in the domes, while facts connected with the events depicted in the respective domes are illustrated on the vaults that support them. The side walls narrate the history of the church and its major saints, and in the mosaics applied to the undersides of the arches that used to support the women's galleries and the vaults that connect the piers we find the everyday saints, the ones closest to the lives of ordinary believers to whom the ground level of the basilica is assigned. All this underlines the profound interdependence of the Christian community present on the earth with that of the saints, the apostles and Christ.

Dome of the Presbytery

Starting from the high altar, the dome of the Presbytery depicts God's promise to humanity that a Savior would be born of a Virgin: the Prophets are distributed around the dome, with the Virgin who will be the mother of God between them and an idealized – as his identity is still unknown – and eternally youthful God at the top. The pendentives contain the four biblical symbols that will later be attributed to the evangelists: the lion, ox, angel and eagle.

Dome of the Ascension

In the central dome we see Christ ascending to heaven after his resurrection. A historical Christ, represented as Man and surrounded by the Apostles who watch his ascent.

At their feet, between the windows of the dome, are set the Human Virtues, along with those deriving from Christ's teachings. The four Evangelists who testified to the actual presence of Christ on earth are portrayed in the pendentives.

The four vaults that support the dome are decorated with *Scenes from the Life of Christ*, from his *Birth* to his *Baptism* (east vault), the *Marriage at Cana* (north vault), the *Temptations in the Wilderness*, the *Entry into Jerusalem*, the *Washing of the Feet* and the *Last Supper* (south vault), and finally from the *Seizure of Christ in the Garden* to the *Ecce Homo, Crucifixion, Resurrection, Descent into Limbo* and the *Visitation of the Apostles*, where he asks Thomas, who has touched his wounds, whether he believes at last (west vault). A question that is addressed to every Christian.

Dome of Pentecost

At the center of the dome is set the throne with the open book of the Gospels and the Spirit of God, awaiting the return of Christ at the end of time. All around, we see the Apostles filled with the Holy Spirit and transfigured before going out to take the message of salvation, the great news that we are the sons of God, to the peoples, represented below them, between the windows of the dome. In the pendentives the Archangels sing the *Sanctus Dominus* of praise for and gratitude toward this God who loves and saves. This iconographic scheme pervades the entire basilica and illustrates this hope for the future, which is a certainty for believers, accompanying and protecting them at every moment of their lives. If they raise their eyes, its harmonious repetition on the "heavenly" vaults reassures them of the love of God.

Sides of the high altar

The *Scenes from the Life of Saint Mark* and the *Retrieval of His Body from Alexandria* underline the fact that the church is dedicated to the evangelist and houses his mortal remains.

Doge's section, south transept

The fasts and prayers of the people, the clergy and the doge are depicted on the west wall, along with the *Finding of the Saint's Body*.

South dome or dome of St. Leonard

Leonard, Blaise, Clement and Nicholas are all what might be called "political" saints for the role that they assume with respect to the doge. Leonard, a king who became a saint, stands for a kind of rule based on the rectitude of the sovereign's treatment of his subjects. Nicholas, saint of the sea, linked Venice to the coasts of the Adriatic and Aegean, where he was widely venerated. Clement, the third pope, indicates the

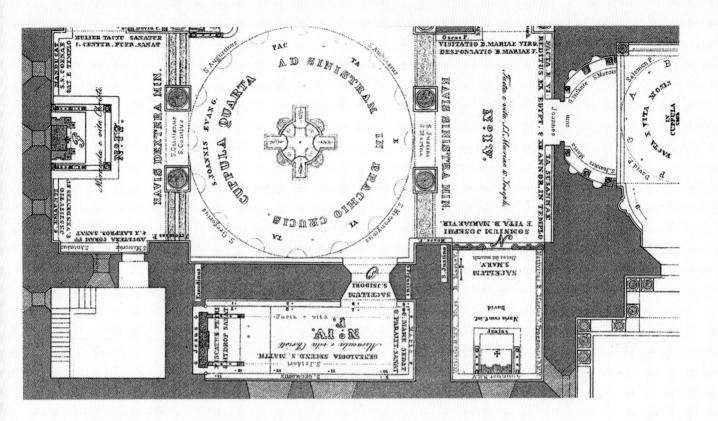

attention and respect paid by the Signoria of Venice to the papacy. Blaise was one of the saints venerated in territories with which the Repubblica Serenissima maintained continuous ties.
In the pendentives we find the female saints Erasma, Euphemia, Dorothy and Thecla.

North dome or dome of St. John

Here the mosaics represent *Scenes from the Life of Saint John the Evangelist*, prototype of the priest. At the center a sort of wind rose indicates the cardinal points and superimposes on them the new reference points of the coming of Christ, who permeates and transforms everything. They are a splendid, concise and to some degree hermetic interpretation of the apotheosis of creation following the birth of Christ.

In the pendentives, the four Doctors of the Western Church: Jerome, Gregory, Augustine and Ambrose.

Walls of the transepts

Scenes from the Life of Christ are depicted on the eastern walls. At the center, in the semidome of the apse, we see the Pantocrator, a majestic figure reworked in 1506. On the western walls opposite the *Scenes from the Life of Christ*, are set *Scenes from the Life of the Virgin*, partly drawn from the Apocryphal Gospels, as the only human being worthy of being placed at the same height opposite Christ. The two lives of Jesus and his Mother have a point of contact, in the promise made by God to Adam and which has its root in Jesse. And on the rear wall of the north transept we find the splendid representation of the *Tree of Jesse*,

which has been described as "the Sistine Chapel of Venice." At its top is set the *Virgin Mary Holding the Child in Her Arms*, the work of Vincenzo Bianchini (1542-52), to a cartoon by Giuseppe Porta, called Salviati.

Nave

Scenes from the lives of the apostles are depicted on the walls and vaults under the dome of Pentecost. In a masterly sequence executed by two or more mosaicists between 1214 and 1220 at the bottom on the southern side, we see *Jesus's Agony in the Garden* with the *Seizure of Jesus* represented at the start of the vault, between the dome of the Ascension and that of Pentecost.

West vault of Pentecost

On the way out, we see the large vault with the *Last Judgment*,

preceded by *Scenes from Revelation* and completed, on the walls, by depictions of heaven and hell. At the exit, in the bowl-shaped vault of the central portal, the narration returns to the theme of Christ the Judge flanked by his mother.

70

G. and L. Kreutz, Plan of Saint Mark's Basilica, lithograph by F. Weifs, Vienna 1843, detail of the north transept

This is the area currently set aside for prayer.

71

Capital of the Crucifix, nave, pier on the left before the crossing

A small altar enclosed in an aedicule with a hexagonal base and a pointed roof, constructed out of precious marble, small columns and capitals. It houses an ancient icon in the shape of a cross, with Christ painted on panel, which according to legend was brought to Venice prior to the booty of the Fourth Crusade. It is said that a madman struck it several times with a dagger in the second half of the 13th century, and that the image bled. The recent restoration carried out by Antonino Rusconi between 1972 and 1975 appears to confirm the presence of damage that could have been inflicted in such a manner. The altar is continually lit up by many votive candles.

72

Iconostasis viewed from the side

From this point of view, even more than from the front, the iconostasis creates the impression of an enclosure. Above the trabeation, the large and recently restored Christ in embossed silver is hemmed in between statues of the Apostles, themselves preceded by figures of the Madonna and St. John the Evangelist, as if they were mediating between the congregation and the sacred area of the presbytery.

Venice in 1807, dates from the thirteenth century. The changes made in the first half of the nineteenth century were carried out for liturgical reasons. To the left of the presbytery we find the apsidal chapel of St. Peter, screened like the matching chapel of St. Clement on the right by a marble iconostasis. Above the architrave is set the *Virgin between Saints Mary Magdalen, Cecilia, Helen and Margaret*, a late fourteenth-century work attributed to the Dalle Masegne brothers. Above the altar we see a marble bas-relief: reassembled in the nineteenth century, it depicts *Saint Peter Adored by Two Procurators* (first half of fourteenth century).

In the left-hand corner at the end of the transept is set the Mascoli Chapel, dedicated since 1618 to the confraternity of the same name, founded in St. Mark's at the beginning of the twelfth century. This originally met in the crypt, then at the altar of St. John, now the altar of the Nikopoia, and finally in the Mascoli Chapel. At the outset it was simply called the *cappella nova*. It dates from the middle of the fifteenth century and is a splendid example of Venetian Gothic. The altar is adorned with statues of the Virgin and Child between Saints Mark and John, the work of Bartolomeo Bon.

Opposite the altar of the Nikopoia stands the Porta della Madonna, the doorway between the north transept and the north arm of the atrium. The mosaic above the door represents *Saint John the Evangelist* and dates from the fourteenth century. On the pier set at the corner with the nave we see the *Madonna with a Rifle*, a nineteenth-century armorial bearing that may have been a votive offering from marines in the Venetian navy who had miraculously survived the Austrian shells that fell on Marghera on May 10, 1849.

73

Chapel of St. Clement, Iconostasis, 14th century
A work attributed to the Dalle Masegne brothers that, together with the iconostasis in the Chapel of St. Peter, completes the splendid "enclosure" of the presbytery. The work dates from the high Gothic period and is characterized by the great quality and preciosity of the marble used. Five statues are set on top: the Madonna and Child in the middle, flanked by Saints Christine, Clare, Catherine and Agnes.

74

Small altar of St. Paul, south pier of the altar of the Nikopoia

The work, dating from the Venetian Renaissance, is refined in its proportions and the statues that adorn it as well as the bas-relief of the marble altar frontal are of high quality. It was commissioned by Doge Cristoforo Moro (1462-71).

75

Small altar of San Giacomo, north pier of the altar of St. Leonard, formerly of the Holy Sacrament

The work, dating from the Venetian Renaissance, is refined in its proportions and the statues that adorn it, as well as the bas-relief of the marble altar frontal, are of high quality. It was commissioned by Doge Cristoforo Moro (1462-71).

76 *right*

Chapel of St. Peter

The chapel to the left of the presbytery, along with that of St. Clement to the right, constitutes a part of the basilica that is worth taking a closer look at, for what it can tell us about the history of the alterations made to the architecture of St. Mark's. The original ceiling of the two chapels, which were certainly part of the first church, has been removed. The height of what remains of the vaults above the floor of the crypt is consistent with hypothetical reconstructions of the first church, based on the position and size of the figures in the mosaic of the *Deposition from the Cross*, found on the southwest pier of the presbytery. All that remains of the ceiling decoration, in both the chapel of St. Peter and that of

St. Clement, are the apsidal bowl-shaped vaults with figures of the saints to whom the chapels are dedicated. In that of St. Peter four Seraphim at the sides are accompanied by the inscription: "This covered head represents the deity. The future life is our hope. The past and the fleeting present are hardly known to us."

77 *following pages*

Representation of the Prayer for Discovery of the Body of Saint Mark, mosaic, second quarter of 13th century, south transept, west wall

Here we find a detailed representation of the basilica's interior. Note the baldachin and the double ambo on the left. The domes on top of the basilica are of the depressed – and therefore Byzantine – type, clad in lead. This mosaic is about fifty years older than the one on the outside, in the bowl-shaped vault of St. Alypius, where the domes appear as tall as they are today.

78 *above*

Representation of the Inventio, the Finding of the Body of Saint Mark, mosaic, second quarter of 13th century, south transept, west wall

This is a different, but equally detailed representation of the interior of St. Mark's Basilica. Note the doge's ambo and the large gilded door at the entrance to the church. Here too the domes that roof the basilica are of the flattened, Byzantine type.

79 *right*

Icon of the Blessed Virgin Nikopoia, altar of the north transept

The icon in the Byzantine style was placed on this altar in 1617, after modifications were made by Tommaso Contin. The icon, also called *Hodegetria* ("she who points the way"), was carried into battle at the head of the army, as *Nikopoia*, "bringer of victory." It is said to date from the 10th century and used to belong to the monastery of St. John the Theologian in Constantinople.

It came to Venice with the booty of the Fourth Crusade (1204). The icon used to be covered with votive jewelry but this was removed after the robbery that took place in 1970, though it still has its old silver frame, modified in the 17th century.

The icon was displayed on the high altar on solemn feast days and at times when Venice was under threat. Along with the small altar of the Crucifix, the icon of the *Blessed Virgin Nikopoia* is the object of constant devotion.

THE ICONOSTASIS OF THE DALLE MASEGNE BROTHERS

Guido Tigler

The presbytery is raised slightly above the crypt, much of which is located below ground. Its front is decorated with small arches carved in bas-relief at the end of the eleventh century. As early as 1094 a sort of iconostasis (or, rather, a *templon*) may have been set on top of these, and some fairly fanciful conjectures have been put forward about it. However, it is likely that it consisted simply of an architrave supported by columns, like that of the chapel on the left which is depicted in a scene of the *Pala Feriale*, or *Weekday Altarpiece*, dating from 1345. Even in the present late Gothic version, which has a structure of the same type but enriched with decorative details and adorned with statues, the screen has a similar character to those of the chancel and the two side chapels of St. Peter and St. Clement. The precious "antique marble" of the panels at the bottom, the clouded red Verona marble of the columns and the once bright colors of the statues, now blackened by the smoke of candles, make it a feast for the eyes. It is a masterpiece of Venetian architecture and sculpture, which was dominated in the last two decades of the fourteenth century by the two brothers who signed the iconostasis: Jacobello and Pier Paolo Dalle Masegne. We can go along with Wolfgang Wolters in assigning the statues of the central part (the mourners at the sides of the cross and the Apostles) to Jacobello, owing to their affinities with some of the figures in the altarpiece of San Francesco in Bologna, begun in 1386. This part bears the inscription-cum-signature of the two brothers, referring to the work as a whole, and the date 1394. The metal crucifix in the middle, on the other hand, is signed, again in 1394, by a certain "Jacobus M(a)g(ist)ri Ma(r)ci Benato." The figures of the lateral iconostases (the Madonna, twice, and female saints), dated 1397, can

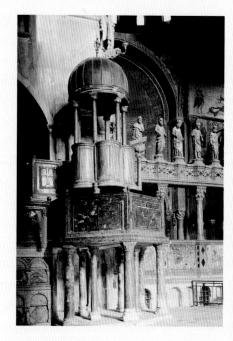

be attributed to Pier Paolo. The Dalle Masegne are also believed to have been responsible for the elegant structures of the two shrines, documented in 1388, but the small figures they contain are the work of assistants.

80 *above*

The left-hand ambo of the iconostasis
Ancient walls from the East (13th century) have been reassembled to form a double ambo: on the first level is set the reading of the Epistles, on the upper level the reading of the Gospels.

81

Foreshortened view of the iconostasis
On top, the statues of the twelve apostles, with the Virgin and St. John the Baptist at the foot of the central cross, in gilded bronze with Christ in embossed silver. The sculptures are the work of Pierpaolo and Jacobello Dalle Masegne (1394). Christ and the figures that adorn the cross are by Jacopo and Marco Bennato.

THE BALDACHIN
Ettore Vio

The baldachin, or ciborium, supported by four columns of alabaster from the East, is the most precious feature of the presbytery. The block, carved into two intersecting tunnel vaults and covered in its entirety with slabs of "verd antique," rests on twelfth-century capitals. In a print made in the first half of the eighteenth century, Antonio Visentini shows it surmounted by a cupola of gilded wood. Statues of Christ between St. Mark and St. John are set on the edge facing the congregation, while the Redeemer (1751) between St. Mark and St. Luke, works dating from the thirteenth century, are placed at the back, facing the apse. The figure of Christ in the middle at the front has been attributed by Anne Markham Schulz to the great sculptor Tullio Lombardo.

The debate over the baldachin has focused primarily on the date and provenance of the four columns. The bas-reliefs that adorn them, while differing in some ways, such as the form of the small arches that enclose the scenes, the type of lettering and the style of the clothing, are basically alike and must come from a single center of production, even if executed by sculptors of varying talent.

In the first half of the twentieth century, scholars like Toesca and Bettini argued that the style of the columns was similar to that of Syrian and Egyptian ivories from the fifth and sixth century, as well as Coptic sculptures. After the Second World War, however, Lucchesi Palli used analogies with Western iconographies and models to claim that that they were more likely to have been produced by a thirteenth-century Venetian workshop.

According to tradition, the columns came from Santa Maria in Canneto and were brought to Venice by Doge Pietro Orseolo II (991-1008) after an expedition to Dalmatia. An authoritative German scholar, Thomas Weigel, has now removed all

82

View of the baldachin

The most sacred place in the basilica, enclosing the high altar that has been left open on its longer sides so that the marble sarcophagus housing the body of St. Mark can be seen. In the background, the *Pala d'oro*, facing the congregation, echoes the splendor of the columns with its repetitive series of small arches enclosing the *cloisonné* enamels. Above, the figure of the *Pantocrator* in the semidome of the apse, a mosaic signed "Petrus 1506."

doubts over the matter and found confirmation of the tradition of their antiquity. Among the elements providing evidence for this and for their transport to the basilica of St. Mark from a previous location are the iconography of the crucifixion, where the figure of Christ is replaced by the symbol of the Mystic Lamb, and the fractures visible on the upper and lower shafts, resulting from the removal of the columns and their adaptation to their new location. Breaks in the inscriptions caused by these fractures have been filled in.

As for the iconography, Weigel cites the decision taken at the Trullan Council held in Constantinople in 692 AD, forbidding the use of the Mystic Lamb in the place of Christ owing to the incapacity of the majority of believers to grasp its purely symbolic value. This did not prevent the Venetians from using the ancient columns, whereas it would certainly have stopped them from carving new ones with an iconography that had been banished from the artistic repertory of the time.

The baldachin is the heart of the basilica and reaches the height of its significance, as the hub of the basilica's message as well as of its history and values, on feast days in honor of the saint, when the gratings around the sarcophagus and its relics are removed and they are covered with red roses, while the *Pala d'oro* gleams in front of the congregation.

83

Baldachin, detail of the carving on one of the four alabaster columns that support the vault

Recent studies have dated the columns, which were used for another purpose before being installed in St. Mark's, to the 7th century. They are decorated with ninety scenes, each accompanied by an inscription engraved on the band that separates one panel from the next. The rear column on the left has *Scenes from the Life of the Virgin*, from her birth to marriage, the front column on the left scenes with the *Virgin and Jesus* and the rear and front columns on the right episodes from the *Life of Jesus*, from the entry into Jerusalem to his glorification in heaven.

84

Antonio Visentini, View of Saint Mark's Basilica, engraving from the early part of the 18th century

At the center we see the presbytery surmounted by the gilded dome that no longer exists. On the right and left sides are the organs that predated the ones made by Callido in 1766, facing one another in the choirs. In the only surviving record of these instruments, the 15th-century organ is on the right, the 16th-century organ on the left. A section of the wooden tribunes, used by the choristers, is visible in the foreground, between the north and south piers of the presbytery.

THE INSCRIPTIONS OF THE MOSAICS

Maria Da Villa Urbani

"A prayer book, an immense illuminated missal bound in alabaster instead of parchment": just one of the many telling images used by John Ruskin in his book *The Stones of Venice* (1852) in an effort to convey his feelings about the basilica of St. Mark, that splendid monument to faith and civilization in the heart of the city he loved most in all the world. When reading this "immense illuminated missal" we should follow the iconographic scheme drawn up for its central nucleus by a medieval theologian in the twelfth century: the story of Christian salvation.

Here we would like to offer the interested visitor an explanation of the inscriptions that accompany each of the many scenes and amplify their spiritual meaning. The majority of these texts, almost all in the Latin tongue and sometimes written in abbreviated epigraphic form, are based on the scriptures of the Old and New Testament and provide a commentary on each scene.

However, there are also numerous prayers and invocations, in typically medieval poetic form (leonine rhyme), inscribed on the arches, semidomes and vaults. Frequently addressed to St. Mark, it appears that they were composed specially for this Venetian church.

As a brief example, we shall choose the area of the central portal leading from the atrium into the church itself. Four niches around the doorway contain figures of the four evangelists in the canonical order: Matthew, Mark, Luke and John. They are considered to be some of the church's oldest mosaics, dating from the end of the eleventh century. A hemistich runs along the upper part of each niche: *Ecclesiae Christi vigiles / sunt quattuor isti / quorum dulce melos / sonat et movet undique coelos* ("These four are sentinels of Christ's church, their sweet song rings out and

moves the heavens everywhere"). Above, a band of smaller size contains the images of eight apostles, also very old, around that of the Virgin. It is to the latter that the inscription running horizontally refers, associating her with the Church in accordance with ancient patristic tradition: *Sponsa Deo gigno natos ex virgine virgo / quos fragiles firmo fortes super aethera mitto* ("Bride of God, ever virgin, she gave birth to children whom she strengthened in their weakness and sent to Heaven"). The prayer on the front of the large semidome above the portal is addressed directly to Mark, the evangelist and patron saint of the city: he is depicted in a sixteenth-century mosaic, dressed in vestments and welcoming the faithful to his church: *Alapis Marce delicta precantibus arce / ut surgant per te factore suo miserante* (O Mark drive away sin from those who join their hands in prayer to you, may they be saved through your intercession and the mercy of God").

Above the portal itself, on the inside, a lunette contains a thirteenth-century mosaic depicting the Virgin Mary and St. Mark interceding on behalf of humanity with Christ, represented as Pantocrator, lord and judge of the universe. However, it is the words from the Gospel according to John, clearly visible on the book, that give us the key we need to interpret the figure of Jesus, as he says of himself: *Ego sum ostium, si quis per me introierit salvabitur et pasqua inveniet* ("I am the door: by me if

85

Dome of the chancel
Mosaic from the first half of the 12th century, executed by Byzantine craftsmen. It marks the beginning of the iconographic sequence, with the series of Prophets recalling God's promise of the salvation of humanity, the *Virgin among the Prophets*, at the center of the dome of Emmanuel.

any man enter in, he shall be saved, and shall go in and out, and find pasture"). At that time the opening through which people entered the church from the outside, it became a clear symbol of the "door" to the kingdom of God, the person of Christ himself.

Finally, looking at the numerous figures of prophets, apostles and saints that throng the undersides of arches, the walls at all heights and the piers of the great vaults, we see that each is accompanied by an inscription giving the figure's name. This is a practice typical of Eastern icons painted on wood, where the name is an essential part of the picture. Nevertheless, as has already been pointed out, the inscriptions are in Latin, showing that Venice, however strongly influenced by Byzantium, lay fully within the sphere of Western culture.

It is only for Jesus Christ and his mother Mary that monograms in Greek are used, as if to underline their superiority.

86

Dome of the Ascension

Mosaic from the last quarter of the 12th century, executed by Byzantine craftsmen. At the center, Christ is lifted up by angels to a starry heaven. Around him, on the ground, the apostles look on. The trees that separate the figures represent the new life.

At the base of the dome, between the windows, the *New Virtues* pointing out the way of the Christian. The mosaic is considered one of the finest examples of Byzantine art in Italy.

SIC ACTVS CHRISTI
SCT MAEV

VIDIT LEVI
ALPHÆI

LIBER FILII
GENE DAV
RAT ID
ONS FILII
IHS ABRA
XPI HAM

87 *on page 118*

Saint Matthew the Evangelist Writing His Gospel, mosaic from the last quarter of the 12th century, dome of the Ascension, northeast pendentive

The mosaic is the work of Byzantine craftsmen. In the background, buildings alluding to places with which the saint is associated. At its foot, the biblical river Gion, symbol of the water of new life to be found in the Gospels.

88 *on page 119*

Saint John the Evangelist Writing His Gospel, mosaic from the last quarter of the 12th century, dome of the Ascension, southwest pendentive

The mosaic is the work of Byzantine craftsmen. In the background, buildings alluding to places with which the saint is associated. At its foot, the biblical river Fison, symbol of the water of new life to be found in the Gospels.

89 *left above*

Saint Luke the Evangelist Writing His Gospel, mosaic from the last quarter of the 12th century, dome of the Ascension, southeast pendentive

The mosaic is the work of Byzantine craftsmen. In the background, buildings alluding to places with which the saint is associated.

90 *left below*

Saint Mark the Evangelist Writing His Gospel, mosaic from the last quarter of the 12th century, dome of the Ascension, northwest pendentive

The mosaic is the work of Byzantine craftsmen. In the background, buildings alluding to places with which the saint is associated.

91

Dome of the Ascension, detail, mosaic from the last quarter of the 12th century

The work of Byzantine craftsmen, the detail shows the segment of the bowl-shaped vault with the Madonna and the Apostles, as well as the Virtues underneath.

Dome of Pentecost

Mosaic from the 1st half of the 12th century
executed by Byzantine craftsmen. Numerous
restorations were carried out in the western
part between the 15th and the 18th century.
At the center the *Hetoimasia* (throne of
judgment) and the dove of the Holy Spirit.
Around them, the Byzantine series of twelve
Apostles, which includes the four Evangelists
and St. Paul. The Evangelists are recognizable
by the book that they hold. Their expressions
are imbued with a new Spirit. Underneath,
between the windows, the peoples who
listened to their preaching, according to the list
in the Acts of the Apostles.

93 *right*

Dome of Pentecost, detail

Mosaic from the first half of the 12th century, executed by Byzantine craftsmen. Pendentive with the image of an Archangel singing the *Sanctus* of praise for and gratitude toward God for the salvation of humanity, which is repeated in the other pendentives.

94 *facing page*

Vault between the dome of the Ascension and the dome of Pentecost

The work of the Master of the Crucifixion, end of 12th century. Of exceptional artistic quality, it is held up by Otto Demus as an example of the highest level attained by the mosaics in the basilica. From south to north, we see the *Kiss of Judas*, the *Ecce Homo*, the *Crucifixion*, the *Women at the Tomb* (remade in the 15th century) at the center, the *Descent into Limbo* and finally the *Incredulity of Thomas*.

95 *following pages*

The Kiss of Judas and Ecce Homo, vault between the dome of the Ascension and the dome of Pentecost, mosaic, 12th century, detail

Otto Demus considers these to be among the finest mosaics in the basilica.

97

The Virgin Mary, mosaic, 13th century, pinakes, south wall of the nave

The *pinakes* are panels of mosaic inserted in the marble facing, a sort of repetition of the iconography of the dome of the chancel at a lower level for the convenience of the congregation, as it is hard to see from the nave. They represent the Prophets, the Virgin and future mother of God and the promised God, the Emmanuel, in the semblance of a young man.

The work of the Master of the Prophets in the *Pinakes*, third decade of the 13th century.

96 *facing page*

Agony in the Garden, mosaic, south wall of the nave

The work of several mosaicists, dating from around 1214–20. Detail of the central part with the figure of Christ at different moments of the *Agony in the Garden of Gethsemane*.

98

The Prophet Micah, mosaic, 13th century, pinakes, north wall of the nave

The work of the Master of the Prophets in the *Pinakes*, third decade of the 13th century.

99

The Promised God, the Emmanuel, mosaic, 13th century, pinakes, north wall of the nave

The work of the Master of the Prophets in the *Pinakes*, third decade of the 13th century.

100 *preceding pages*

Vault of the Apocalypse and the Last Judgment

The mosaic that was set on the vertical wall closing the sacred space prior to construction of the large vault has suffered from the structural deterioration of the vault. Ever since the middle of the 19th century attempts have been made to renovate it, following interventions to consolidate the structure. The mosaicist Giovanni Moro made drawings of the 16th-century mosaic, but he ran into legal problems and the board of trustees was forced to dismiss him and make use of cartoons by the then director of the Accademia di Belle Arti, the Austrian Karl von Blaas, who received the commission directly from the government. This was in the years 1860-61, when Austria started to make an annual contribution to the upkeep of the basilica. A more sensitive attitude, advocated by the trustee Pietro Saccardo, prevailed and Blaas's mosaics were never executed. Instead a decision was taken to go back to the designs and skills of the mosaicist Giovanni Moro, as soon as Venice was annexed to the kingdom of Italy in October 1866.

101 *above*

Hell, mosaic, vault of the Judgment

Mosaic at the north base of the vault. Executed to a design by Maffeo da Verona (17th century), it is a splendid representation of the souls of the damned. The large cartoon (in practice a painted canvas) by Maffeo da Verona has survived.

102 *facing page*

Martyrdom of Saint John, mosaic, detail, baptistery, north lunette at the base of the dome of the Angels

The mosaic was executed by the Venetian workshop of the 14th century (1345-54). Detail of Salome with the head of St. John. The fixity of the scene produces a highly dramatic effect: there is a feeling of terror at what has happened. Salome seems to be frozen to the spot.

THE TESSELLATED FLOOR OF ST. MARK'S

Renato Polacco

The modifications that had to be made to the structure in order to keep the evangelist's tomb in its original, ninth-century location, and to the iconography to suit the use of the building as a State chapel, mean that there are differences from the *Apostoleion* in Constantinople, which the Venetians had used as a model for the basilica. Nevertheless, it retains all the basic features of Byzantine ecclesiastical architecture. In addition to the Greek-cross plan and five domes, the principle of the dichotomy between the earthly zone (wall and floors) and the heavenly part (vaults and domes) has been respected. Their different purposes and functions are underlined by the use of different facing materials, or rather by emphasizing the spatial effect created through a suitable decoration of the walls. The upper part of the building assumes an exclusively and evidently celestial connotation, and thus a metaphysical one, through the light reflected from the tesserae made of glass, covered with gold leaf or painted a variety of colors, intended to symbolize the light of Paradise or to carry the richness and brightness of the individual figures to the limits of the intelligible. The lower part, on the other hand, is given a mundane character by the solidity of the marble on the walls (even though this is richly colored, but in duller shades, and covered with geometric designs) and the tessellated floor, made by the techniques known as *opus sectile* and *opus tessellatum*. The overall impression is one of veiled luminosity, a pale reflection on earth of the light of Heaven and a schematic adumbration of the vision of Paradise presented in the mosaics of the domes and ceilings.

In the floor of St. Mark's we find the type of mosaic work known as *opus sectile* (where the patterns are made from pieces

103
Floor of the nave, executed in opus tessellatum

A technique that involved preparing individual pieces of marble of the size and color necessary to create the frames that surrounded the area underneath particular structures and elements of the basilica's roof. These frames had angular shapes, rhomboid or polygonal. They were often used to enclose slabs of marble, as in the case of the enormous area known as "the sea" underneath the crossing, made up of twelve large slabs of Proconnesus marble.

104
Antonio Visentini, Floor of the Basilica, original drawing, 1725-30

The drawing is made on a scale of about 1:100 and in pen and sepia ink. It is the earliest detailed representation of the floor of the basilica. Visentini made two attempts to prepare the copperplate for printing, but was unable to finish the work owing to its technical difficulty. Other representations followed, including a whole collection of drawings tinted with watercolor by Antonio Pellanda, the technician "supervising" work on the basilica in the middle of the 19th century. Another drawing was made in 1881, on a scale of 1:50, by the architect Nicolò Moretti and printed in several plates. The drawings differ from one another in a number of details, something that suggests the existence of successive modifications.

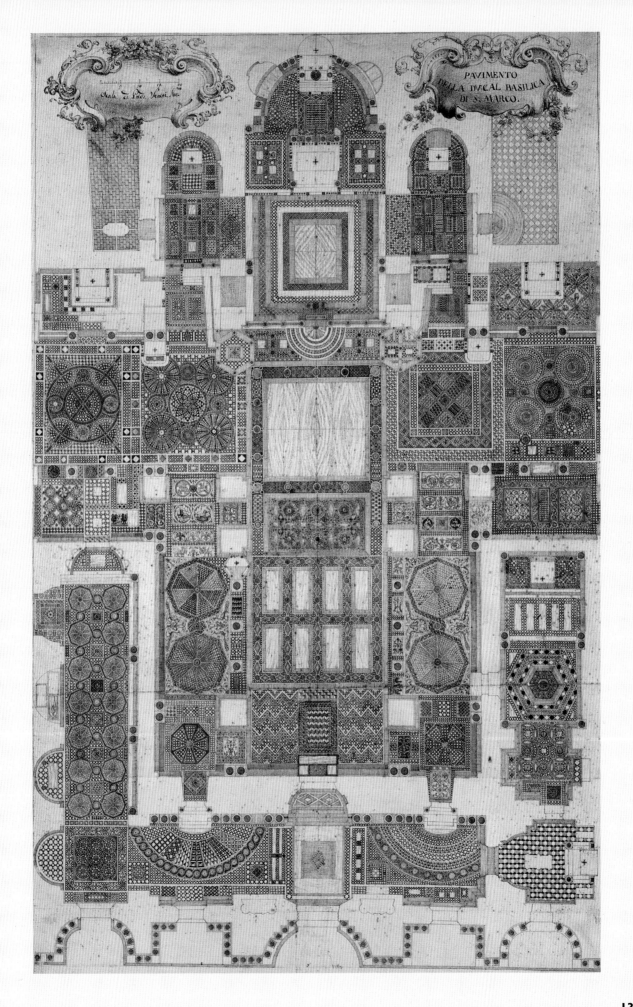

of marble cut into shapes and in a variety of colors) as well as the one called *opus tessellatum* (where tiny pieces of marble or enamel obtained by tapping the material with a chip hammer are used to create floral or animal figures), though the former is much more widely used than the latter. Both techniques originated in ancient times, as is documented in Varro, Vitruvius and Pliny, and *opus tessellatum* was extensively employed in the early Christian and early medieval buildings of the Adriatic region. The early and mid Byzantine period showed a preference for *opus sectile*, as is evident from churches like Hagia Sophia in Constantinople, that of the Greek monastery of Hosios Loukas, near Delphi, and the Nea Moni on the island of Chios. The use of both techniques in St. Mark's Basilica testifies to the ample resources of the duchy, able not only to afford the huge amount of precious marble, indispensable for its qualities of hardness and color, required to lay a flooring that covers a total of 2099 square meters, but also to hire skilled craftsmen who, in all probability,

105

Floor in opus sectile located at the entrance to the basilica, called the Porta di San Pietro, detail

The design represents an icosahedron. It is attributed to Paolo Uccello, active in the basilica between 1425 and 1433.

106 *following pages*

Floor, right-hand aisle, detail

Octagons linked by circles adorn the right-hand (original) and left-hand aisles (relaid in the second half of the 19th century). The decoration is embellished with two pairs of peacocks, a Christian symbol of the Resurrection.

like the architects and mosaicists, were brought to Venice from Constantinople or from Byzantine Greece.

The floor is made up of panels of different sizes, decorated with geometric or figurative motifs. Some of the more brightly-lit areas, such as the ones under the domes of Pentecost and the Ascension, are covered by large slabs of Proconnesus marble.

The patterns are laid out in a regular manner and wherever possible adhere to the principles of symmetry. The nave is decorated with a series of fairly linear designs. Near the entrance we find a large rectangle adorned with a herringbone pattern and including a smaller rectangle in the middle with a similar decoration. In the next panel two rows of four large rectangular slabs of Proconnesus marble are set inside elegant frames of diamonds and circles with red borders. This is followed, as we head toward the presbytery, by a large rectangle with two rows of polychrome rhombuses and wheels, separated by four squares alternating with three rhombuses. Then, under the dome of the Ascension, we come to the "sea" of large slabs of Proconnesus marble.

Each arm of the transept contains two large squares. The ones in the northern arm are both decorated with a quincunx of five large Byzantine wheels, separated from one another by four smaller ones. In the southern arm a pattern of diamonds surrounded by a frame also made up of diamonds is followed, further to the south, by a quincunx of four wheels.

The aisles are each decorated with a square including an octagon, followed to the east by a pair of similar figures. The spaces in between are filled with two pairs of peacocks set alongside a cantharus (a two-handled drinking cup) from which elegant shoots of vegetation emerge (the

two pairs of peacocks in the right-hand or southern aisle stand out for the brilliant colors of the enamel tesserae and the refinement of their execution, an effect enhanced by the fact that they have been preserved almost intact).

The floor of the presbytery has a marble panel at the center opening like a book and surrounded by seven motifs, two rectangles subdivided to form crosses at the sides of the altar and, behind the *Pala d'oro*, a large rectangle framed by braided bands and flanked by two sunburst patterns that stretch as far as the semicircle of the walls.

In the northern atrium an elongated rectangle inscribed with two rows of seven octagons linked by braided ribbon is preceded by a square with three rows of three circles each. The western narthex has geometric patterns of marble at the center (tradition has it that the one in the middle marks the point where Pope Alexander and Frederick Barbarossa met to draw up the treaty of Venice in 1177), flanked by two semicircles. The baptistery is dominated by a large hexagon, with the font at its center, while the floor of the western part is covered with eight circles arranged around a square.

Into this rigorously geometric scheme are inserted symbolic birds and animals and floral elements, enriching and completing a carpet of mosaics that seems to lead us through its allegories as if we were on a pilgrimage of faith. A pilgrimage whose stages are laid down by an iconographic program that we now find extremely complicated, but which was much more easily comprehensible to the people of the Middle Ages.

While there are numerous examples of mosaic floors with geometric designs in the upper Adriatic region, from Aquileia (*tessellatum*) to Grado (*tessellatum*), Torcello (*tessellatum* and *sectile*), Murano

(*sectile* and *tessellatum*), Pomposa and Ravenna, that of St. Mark's stands out for the magnificence, preciosity and rarity of the marble employed, imported from the East, the West and even North Africa, for the splendor of the enamel tesserae and for the variety of the scenes (funerals of foxes, peacocks and other animals), either derived from medieval symbolism and literature or inspired by Eastern and Western fabric designs.

107

Floor in opus sectile made out of red porphyry and green serpentine

Floor located at the junction between the north transept and nave. The "wheel" motifs are executed with particular skill. The large one at the center is attributed to the mosaicist Giacomo Pasterini, who took ten years over the work in the first half of the 17th century. An interesting feature of the pieces of marble is the shape that they take on with wear: in the metamorphic marbles this happens faster at the edges, producing a convex surface, while in the sedimentary ones most of the wear occurs at the center, resulting in a concave surface.

THE CRYPT

Ettore Vio

Underneath the presbytery lies the crypt. This is where the body of Mark the Evangelist was kept for centuries. The crypt is divided into a nave and two aisles, each with an apse. The nave is located under the presbytery, while the right-hand aisle lies beneath the chapel of St. Clement and the left-hand one under the chapel of St. Peter.

You descend to the crypt by means of one of the two staircases located to the left and right of the presbytery, opposite the ones leading to the two side chapels. The crypt has another space to the west: called the "retrocrypt," it is located about midway underneath the area of the crossing and its height does not exceed 1·75 m. The floor of the crypt, laid to a design by Giovanni Battista Meduna at the time of the restoration in 1870, is 36 cm higher than that of the retrocrypt. The former is 20 cm below sea level, and the latter 56.

The crypt is roofed with tunnel vaults built out of intersecting bricks of the Roman type, reaching a maximum height of 2·45 m. They are supported by fifty-six small columns with Veneto-Byzantine capitals that have been dated to the eleventh century. Six of these ring the mortuary chapel that used to house the body of St. Mark and are of finer workmanship. The mortuary chapel consists of a massive slab of Verona marble, about 40 cm thick and 2·5 m on a side, supported at the corners by four columns of Greek cipolin marble, topped by simple rough-hewed capitals of Egyptian green marble. The area of the mortuary chapel is surrounded by Veneto-Byzantine plutei, also from the eleventh century. Inside the mortuary chapel we find a finely-worked altar frontal in the place where the faithful used to come to place objects and pieces of cloth in contact

with the tomb of their patron saint and then take them away as mementos of their visit. The various calamities that have struck the basilica, such as earthquakes and fires, did not leave the crypt unscathed. Some of the capitals and a few of the altar-frontals have had to be replaced.

A marble altarpiece carved with five figures in high relief was set up at the front of the mortuary chapel of St. Mark in 1494. It represents the Virgin and Child flanked by Saints Peter, Mark, Catherine and Hedwig. With the recent restoration work carried out to clear the mortuary chapel completely, the altarpiece has been moved into the left-hand aisle.

From the twelfth century onward the crypt was the seat of the confraternity of the Mascoli.

In 1563 the Venetians, concerned about the rise in sea level and the bradyseism that was causing the city itself to sink lower and lower, attempted to solve the problem by raising the floor 30 cm. However, the continual rise in the sea level put an end to any hope of being able to go on using this ancient part of the basilica, where the mortal remains of St. Mark were kept.

In 1580 the entrances to the crypt were walled up, and it remained closed for almost three centuries.

Two explorations were carried out, one in the seventeenth century and one in the eighteenth: the water level at high tide was measured, reaching around 40 cm in both cases, and material that had not been considered worth saving at the time the crypt was walled up was removed. It was only after Napoleon's transfer of the basilica to the patriarch of Venice in 1807 that serious thought was given to redressing the situation. At once Patriarch Gamboni, followed by his successor Pirker,

devoted study and effort to the problem of recovering St. Mark's body. In 1825 Leonardo Manin published two volumes on the survey that was carried out, describing the marble sarcophagus and the body of the saint. A small box was found alongside the wooden coffin housing the holy remains: among other things, it contained the date on which the body had been placed in the sarcophagus, inscribed on a sheet of lead and corresponding to October 8, 1094. The description was accompanied by several drawings, illustrating the objects found as well. It was Patriarch Pirker who had the sarcophagus removed and positioned immediately above its previous location, under the high altar but at a level where it was safe from flooding. But it was not until Venice was annexed to the kingdom of Italy in 1868 that work began on reclamation of the crypt itself.

Success was immediate and this action, strongly supported by the new state, the kingdom of Italy, through the collaboration of Prefect Torelli and Patriarch Trevisanato, was greeted with enthusiasm by the young people of the city and by all those who had placed their hopes for the preservation and appreciation of the history, faith and deeds of the ancient Venetians in the restoration of the basilica. In 1890-91 the new *proto* Pietro Saccardo decided to use what was considered the best binding material of the time, portland cement, and the "retrocrypt" was reopened. The work proved effective and succeeded in keeping the crypt dry throughout the first half of the twentieth century. After the Second World War, an acceleration in the rate of subsidence of the ground as well as the rise in sea level led to infiltration of water through both

the floor and the walls. The process reached its peak with the flood of November 4, 1966.

As well as permitting examination of the line where the vaults were broken to carry out the foundation work in 1063, the restoration has also allowed an evaluation of the modifications that were made to the vaulting system above those foundations. The date of the first intervention, that of the mortuary chapel, corresponds to that of the construction of the church in 829-32. Work on the foundations of the present basilica commenced in 1063. As the vaults were built between these two dates – in fact they have partially destroyed the columns of the chapel and have in turn been modified to permit insertion of the new

foundations – this can only have happened on the one occasion of historical importance for the basilica, the burning of the church during a revolt against Doge Pietro Candiano IV in 976. During the reconstruction, a fireproof cavity was installed to protect the body of the saint: the outside of it is visible as the vault built out of bricks with a thickness of 40 cm. The present level of the "retrocrypt" is the same as the original one of the crypt before it was raised in 1563. It was only with the construction of the present basilica that the space, which previously opened freely onto the church, was reduced to a sub-confessio in the reconstruction after the fire of 976. It did not become a true crypt until the present basilica was built.

Now reclaimed and fitted with new lighting and ventilation systems, the crypt can be visited on request and is used for special religious functions.

108

View of the crypt, the mortuary chapel that contained the body of St. Mark until 1811

Note the ancient supporting columns of the mortuary chapel, the characteristic roof with tunnel vaults in brick and the enclosure of the central area built out of Veneto-Byzantine marble altar frontals, many of which have been replaced.

143

THE CHAPELS

Ettore Vio

Particular significance is attached to the spaces at the sides of the main structure of the basilica, which are used as votive and subsidiary chapels.

At the end of the north transept, a wooden door faced with bronze and fitted with arched gratings is thought to date from the fourth century. It leads into the chapel of St. Isidore, a simple but suggestive space that is richly adorned with marble facings on the walls. In a lunette with a pointed arch above the altar is set the sarcophagus containing the mortal remains of the Roman soldier and saint, brought to Venice from Chios in 1125.

The architecture of the chapel dates from considerably later, the fourteenth century. The ceiling is covered entirely with mosaics, including the soffits of the windows. They represent scenes from the saint's life and martyrdom. An image of Christ seated on a throne between St. Mark and St. Isidore is set above the altar. The long inscription underneath gives an account of the transport of the saint's body from Chios to Venice by Doge Domenico Michiel, as well as the construction of the chapel as the saint's tomb, begun by Doge Andrea Dandolo and finished by Doge Giovanni Gradenigo in 1355.

What is now the baptistery was created from what used to be the portico decorated with a fresco of the *Ascension* (the feast day was formally celebrated in Venice from 990 AD onward) in the *giesia dei putti*, the first place used for baptism. It was completed in its present form by Doge Giovanni Soranzo (1312-28). The mosaic decoration (1343-54) was carried out by a local workshop and is one of the most significant surviving examples of the Venetian school of mosaic. On the walls we see the cycle of the *Life of Saint John the Baptist* from his birth to his decapitation, while the *Story of Salvation* is represented on the vault of the entrance and the two cupolas, in a similar fashion to that of the cycle in the large domes of the basilica (with the prophets who foresaw the coming of Christ on the vault, Christ sending out the apostles to baptize the peoples of the world, in the central cupola over the font installed by Sansovino, and Christ in glory among angels in the cupola above the altar). Among the mosaics, it is worth singling out the *Baptism of Christ*, showing the first meeting between St. John the Baptist and Christ, the *Dance of Salome* at Herod's banquet and the splendid *Crucifixion* on the eastern wall, behind the altar, in which we see not only the

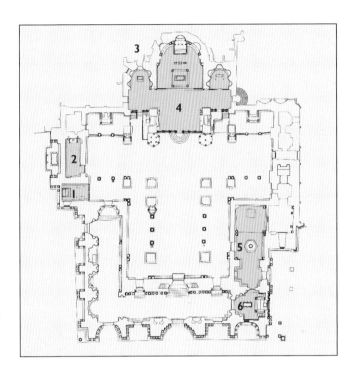

109

Chapel of St. Isidore, view of the altar with the sarcophagus of the saint

This is a 14th-century work, built during the rule of Andrea Dandolo, in the years of the great plague that swept across Europe from east to west, killing up to half of the population. The chapel, probably the right-hand aisle of the ancient church of San Teodoro, is adorned with a cycle of mosaics covering the entire ceiling. It has a highly unitary character and, along with the baptistery and the Mascoli Chapel, constitutes one of the three "Gothic" gems in the originally Byzantine basilica. In the years 1885-86 the *proto* Pietro Saccardo brought it back into use, restoring the splendid mosaics and sculptures.

It is now reserved exclusively for prayer. It is used to house the Communion bread and wine and Mass is celebrated there on weekday mornings.

110

Plan of the basilica showing the location of the chapels

1. Mascoli Chapel

2. chapel of St. Isidore

3. sacristy

4. area of the crypt (under the presbytery)

5. baptistery

6. Zen Chapel

111

Pendentive with Saint Athanasius, baptistery, central dome

Forming part of the iconography of the baptistery, the mosaics represent the *Doctors of the Church*, those of the East – Athanasius, John Chrysostom, Gregory of Nazianzus and Basil – and those of the West – Ambrose, Gregory, Augustine and Jerome. The central dome has been partially restored, with the replacement of some of the heads of the Apostles and the people undergoing baptism. The lines of division between the old mosaics and the ones remade in the second half of the 19th century pass through the base of the dome, in the southwest corner. The figure of St. Athanasius is completely original.

112

Pendentive with Saint Basil, baptistery, central dome

The mosaic of *Saint Basil*, in the southwest pendentive of the central dome, has been completely reconstructed. Here too there is a marked difference in style and quality between the image of St. Basil and the original one of St. Athanasius in the northwest pendentive.

113-114 *left*

Saint Luke and Saint Matthew, mosaics, 14th and 19th century, baptistery, west supporting arch of the central dome

The arch is decorated with the figures of the four Evangelists. Half of the arch underwent considerable alterations during the restoration work of 1865-75. The mosaics in the southern part were completely replaced.

A comparison of the heads of St. Matthew (1875) and St. Luke (1345-54), at the south and north base of the arch respectively, reveals the difference in quality between the original mosaic and the one executed in the 19th century.

115 *right*

General view of the baptistery

The baptistery, once the *giesia dei putti*, is a special area of the basilica, separate from the rest of the church right from the outset and with its own entrance from the outside. In its present form, given to it by Doges Giovanni Soranzo († 1328) and Andrea Dandolo († 1354), it is made up of an antebaptistery, enclosed by a vault, and the baptistery proper with the font at the center and the altar in the eastern part. There are two domes, one over the area of the font and one over the altar. The iconography develops two predominant themes: *Scenes from the Life of Saint John the Baptist* on the walls and *Scenes from the Life of Christ* on the vault and domes.

Virgin Mother and St. John the Baptist, but also St. Mark, Doge Dandolo, who promoted the work, and the State Chancellor Rafaino Caresini.

The baptistery contains a number of other elements, such as the tombs of Doge Giovanni Soranzo (1328) and Doge Andrea Dandolo (1354). The altar is set on top of a block of granite and has an inscription that has never been translated. Tradition has it that this was the stone from which Christ gave the Sermon on the Mount, brought here from Tyre by the Venetians. Recent restoration work on the base of this ponderous mass, 2·5 m on a side and 60 cm thick, has revealed a system of drains underneath. They probably served to collect water from a tub used for baptism by immersion.

The sacristy of St. Mark's now consists of two large spaces: the first is the sacristy proper, which was almost doubled in size by the *proto* Giorgio Spavento in the years following 1486, so that it stretched as far as the front onto the Palazzo canal; the other is the space of the ancient church of San Teodoro, entered through a doorway of modest proportions. Religious services are still held in the church of San Teodoro today.

Between 1500 and 1530 the ceiling of the sacristy was adorned with a mosaic that is considered the last example of the traditional type, in which gold is still the primary component of the decoration. The image is in the Renaissance style, with ancient Roman motifs set alongside the large cross bearing the figure of Christ and saints. The mosaics in the lunettes on the walls, located above the marble facing, represent apostles, prophets and saints to designs by the young Titian, who took a completely new approach with respect to the mosaics on the ceiling. Each figure has a lunette to itself and stands out against the gold ground without blending into it, creating a new sense of depth in a type of decoration that had previously been confined to expressing itself in two dimensions. A *Madonna and Child* to a design attributed to Lorenzo Lotto is placed above the entrance.

The altar frontals and inlaid cabinets in the eastern part of the sacristy were made by the brothers Antonio and Paolo Mola from Mantua and are of great significance. There are twenty-one altar frontals and twelve cabinet doors with themes that display a new formal style in the architecture of the cities represented and depict the principal objects in use at the time by scientists, priests and musicians. The altar frontals in the second part of the sacristy are designed by Jacopo

Sansovino and have a simple structure, decorated with pilaster strips and concluded by architraves of classical proportions.

The Zen chapel was built to house the tomb of Cardinal Zen, in accordance with the terms of his last will and testament, which left a substantial legacy to the republic on condition that he be buried in St. Mark's. The Zen Chapel is formed out of the recess that used to contain the door known as the *Porta da Mar*. On its semidome we see a Virgin and Child and prophets with Christ Emmanuel, while the vault, added at a later date, is adorned with mosaics depicting *Scenes from the Life of Saint Mark* up until his martyrdom. In 1501 a marble transenna was built on the outer edge of this, with a window above it that forms a backdrop to an altar with bronze columns, called the altar of the Madonna della Scarpa, or Madonna with the Shoe. Representing St. Peter and St. John the Baptist as well, it is the work of Antonio Lombardo. The cardinal's sarcophagus is also made of bronze and has the figure of the deceased sculpted in high relief on the lid. The chapel was restored at the beginning of 1980 and communicates directly with the atrium and baptistery. Both the large gate with late Roman gratings and the bronze door leading to the baptistery have been restored recently.

116

Zen Chapel

The former *Porta da Mar*, or "sea door," closed up by the construction of an external transenna out of panels of Greek marble and a large upper window, now houses the "altar of the Madonna of the Shoe," carved by Antonio Lombardo. The figure of the Virgin is flanked by St. Peter and St. John the Baptist and enclosed by a baldachin with columns that have bases made out of Parian marble and shafts of bronze. The baldachin itself is made of bronze over a wooden structure and has a relief depicting the Eternal Father and the Holy Spirit on its ceiling. At the center of the chapel stands the sarcophagus of Cardinal Giovanni Battista Zen with a sculpture of the deceased dressed in his cardinal's robes in full relief on top. The engraver and sculptor Paolo Savin collaborated with Antonio Lombardo and took over from him to complete the work. The bronzes were cast by Pietro Campanato.

THE INLAID CABINETS IN THE SACRISTY

Umberto Daniele

The wooden inlaid work in the sacristy constitutes one of the most remarkable late fifteenth-century cycles of images to have survived in Venice, very close to the dreamlike visions of Carpaccio. Three of the cabinets, set against the walls that back onto the Rio di Palazzo, are decorated with fifteen still lifes, located inside a *trompe-l'oeil* closet with open doors. Above them a tall architectural structure encloses twenty-one urban views. Some of them have a scene or miracle from the life of St. Mark in the foreground: these are the earliest representations of the hagiography of St. Mark in the modern era, drawn from the basilica's *Legendary* (twelfth-fifteenth century). The other views depict an ideal version of the city, framed by a triumphal arch, in which the most recent sacred and profane works of architecture (the façades of Santa Maria dei Miracoli and San Zaccaria, the Scala del Bovolo) are presented as emblems of the *renovatio urbis* promoted by Doge Agostino Barbarigo. Likewise, the still lifes do not represent just the conventional church vestments and ornaments, but also musical instruments, fountains and other Neoplatonic symbols of the harmony of the cosmos. Many famous inlayers, such as the Canozi brothers from Lendinara, or the Olivetan monk Sebastiano da Rovigno, have been suggested by historians as authors of the work. In reality the precious carvings (*c.* 1493-96) are probably by the Florentine Tommaso Astorio, while the majority of the inlays (*c.* 1497-1500) are the signed work of the Mantuan brothers Antonio (*c.* 1465-*c.* 1532) and Paolo Mola (*c.* 1475-1545), who were also responsible for the inlays in the chancel of the Pavia Charterhouse (1489) and Isabella d'Este's Grotto in Mantua (1506). In 1523 the cycle was completed by the Olivetan Vincenzo da Verona (*c.* 1480-1531), with

the assistance of the Jesuit Pietro da Padova (*c.* 1500-1559). Originally they also included the inlays of a large bench, used to close off the area of the cabinets but now lost.

117

Sacristy, design of one of the doors of the cabinets under the altar frontals

When the fifteen doors are open they reveal representations of articles used for scientific, religious and musical purposes by the learned and refined men of the Renaissance.

118

Inlays of the altar frontals in the sacristy

The work of the brothers Antonio and Paolo Mola of Mantua (1496–1506), the twenty-one altar frontals represent views of cities: genuine proposals of urban design, based on application of the new canons and models of Renaissance architecture and depicted by means of the technique of placing a perspective view inside an arched frame, an imaginary window, through which we can enjoy the inlaid scene. In the photograph, a view of the lagoon front with a type of cargo vessel, armed for defense, known as a "Venetian carrack," represented with the emphasis on a dimension that involves and determines the urban scene. Many of the inlays depict *Miracles of Saint Mark.*

THE ANGELS IN THE BAPTISTERY

Antonio Niero

The cupola above the altar is split into three concentric circles. In the central one Christ is giving his blessing, flanked by two seraphim with six wings as described in the book of Isaiah (6, 1-2). The second circle is supported by nine angels, each holding a torch, a succinct reference to the nine hosts or choirs of angels of which Christ is the Lord according to the doctrine of the New Testament.

In the third circle, at the base of the dome, we see nine angelic choirs, in keeping with the specific doctrine put forward in the thirty-fourth homily of Pope Gregory the Great (540-604), which in turn harks back to Pseudo-Dionysius the Areopagite's *De Hierarchia Celesti* ("On the Celestial Hierarchy," fifth century), one of the fullest treatments of the subject. Each choir is represented by a single angel in the role of choirmaster. The iconographic interpretation of the nine choirs can proceed from the ninth to the first (from bottom to top) or in the opposite direction, as we suggest to the visitor. The point of reference is provided by the Seraphim, the ninth choir, located near the cross of the altar below. At its opposite end are set the Angels and Archangels, who are holding souls of the righteous, swathed like mummies. Those held by the Angels have their heads covered, while the heads of the ones held by the Archangels are bare, perhaps to indicate that they are people of greater authority, as Archangels would be expected to be given more prestigious charges. They are followed in a counterclockwise direction by the Virtues, with a corpse near a stream of water flowing from the rock and a devilish figure in the background on the top of a pillar of fire. Next come the Powers, with the choirmaster binding a demon, and the Principalities with the choirmaster brandishing a sword, seated on a throne.

At this point it is necessary to go back to the Angels at the top again and, moving in a clockwise direction this time, look first at the Dominions, where the choirmaster is weighing a soul in the form of a naked youth, while struggling with a demon who is trying to gain possession of the soul by adding heavy stones to make the pan of the scales tip in his direction. On the opposite side of the circle are ranged the last three angelic choirs, i.e. the Seraphim on the left with their choirmaster seated on a throne and, matching them on the right, the Thrones with their leader seated on the celestial globe, wearing a royal crown and holding a lilied scepter. These two choirs form a triad with a ten-winged Cherub in the middle. Around him runs the inscription *sciencie plenitudo* ("fullness of knowledge").

Before attempting an iconographic interpretation of the whole, it should be said that the program for these figures seems to have been drawn up by Doge Andrea Dandolo (1343-54), who intended the baptistery to serve as his mortuary chapel. In fact the iconography of the Angels, or rather of the Archangels, recalls the offertory of the Mass said for the souls of the dead, in use since the ninth century. In this God is asked to let the Archangel Michael lead the souls into the holy light, after Christ has freed them by raising them from their sufferings in the deep lake, shown here in the cave underneath where a number of souls are waiting their turn to be set free. The images linked to the choir of the Virtues sum up their function, i.e. that of working miracles. Hence the allusion to the corpse they are protecting and the water flowing from the rock, a reference to the miracle wrought at Mont Saint-Michel on the coast of Brittany, as well as to salvation from Hell (devil amidst the flames). Amongst the Powers, the devil about to be bound with a long chain takes

its inspiration directly from the text of Revelation (20, 1-3). Although this speaks only of a generic angel, it is intended as a reminder of the holy choir's function of restraining the forces of evil in their assault upon Christian believers. The fact that the Principalities are seated on a throne is meant to show that they are the chiefs (*principes*) of the lesser angels who ensure that divine orders are promptly executed. The image of the weighing of the soul and the struggle with the demon in the Dominions underlines the strength that they impart to the faithful through their participation in divine decrees, although the scene of St. Michael as *psychopomp* (weigher of souls) was a common one in medieval iconography. The Thrones seated on the starry globe symbolize their mission of supporting the throne of God and keeping human beings steady on the good path. The fullness of the knowledge of God represented in the Cherubim serves to enlighten our ignorance, while the Seraphim with their classic six wings, set at the very top of the ranks, are burning with love for God, with the aim of inflaming human hearts as well. The inscription *sciencie plenitudo* is taken straight from the aforementioned thirty-fourth homily of St. Gregory the Great. He points out that fullness of knowledge, according to St. Paul, is fullness of Love, and thus the ten wings of the Cherub allude to the perfect number ten, or rather to the Ten Commandments which epitomize the love of God and our fellow human beings. Dandolo may have drawn this iconography directly from St. Gregory's long homily, though he must have taken the episode of the Virtues with the water flowing from the rock from the *Golden Legend* of Jacobus de Varagine (1208-98). St. Gregory presents the choirs of angels in the following order: Angels, Archangels, Virtues, Powers, Principalities (represented in exactly the same sequence in the mosaic, starting from the left), Dominions, Thrones, Cherubim and Seraphim (set opposite the Principalities on the right of the mosaic). Support for Dandolo's preference for St. Gregory's text is provided by the representation of the saint in the pendentive on the right, in association with the *sciencie plenitudo*.

119 *top (thrones)*

Baptistery, dome of the Angels, detail of the Thrones

The angel that denotes the choir of the Thrones is represented with a crown on his head and a scepter to indicate his power. He is seated on a throne of stars.

120 *bottom (angels)*

Baptistery, dome of the Angels, detail of the Angels and Archangels

A unique and highly suggestive image showing the two figures facing one another, taking a direct interest in the lives of human beings.

121 *following pages*

Baptistery, dome of the Angels

One of the few complete representations of the angelic hierarchy. In sequence, we find personifications, accompanied by their principal functions, of the Angels that watch over the soul during its earthly existence, the Archangels that present the soul of the deceased to God, the Virtues, the Powers, the Principalities, the Seraphim, the Cherubim (the angel portrayed with ten wings and the inscription *sciencie plenitudo*), the Thrones and the Dominions. Original mosaic from 1343-54.

THE MOSAICS OF THE MASCOLI CHAPEL

Maria Da Villa Urbani

The *cappella nova* of the Madonna, also called the Mascoli Chapel, was built at the behest of Doge Francesco Foscari in 1430, as a mark of his gratitude to the Virgin for having survived an attempt on his life by political opponents. The name by which it is most commonly known derives from the ancient confraternity of the Mascoli, whose first seat had been in the crypt. When this became impracticable in the second half of the sixteenth century, the confraternity moved to the chapel of St. John in the north transept and then, in 1618, when the image of the Madonna known as the *Nikopoia* was given a definitive home there on a sumptuous baroque altar, was assigned the small chapel of the Madonna by Doge Antonio Priuli.

In 1430 Doge Foscari, to fulfil his vow, decided to restructure this space, originally the vestibule to the adjoining chapel of St. Isidore, with which it communicated through a door that is now walled up, but still visible. The room, which is small in size (7·11 x 4·21 m in plan; 7·95 m in height), is completely open on the side facing the church and has an altar set against the back wall: this is decorated with a marble frontal with two angels, holding a censer and kneeling at the sides of the cross. The altarpiece, in pale marble with traces of gilding, consists of three narrow shell-shaped niches surmounted by inflected arches adorned with foliage. Inside the niches, separated by spiral columns terminating in tall polygonal spires, are set three splendid examples of Gothic sculpture that display the innovations introduced by Venetian culture as well as Tuscan influences. They represent the Madonna and Child, St. Mark and St. John the Evangelist, in an echo of the iconography of the mosaic in the bowl-shaped vault over the nearby door, leading from the atrium to the north transept and

the chapel dedicated to St. John the Evangelist, traditionally associated with the figure of the Madonna, who was entrusted to him by the dying Jesus on the cross, according to the account in his Gospel (19, 26-7).

The mosaic decoration of the chapel's tunnel vault and rear wall, executed around the middle of the fifteenth century, depicts five episodes from the *Life of the Virgin Mary* drawn from the canonical Gospels of Matthew and Luke and from the apocryphal Gospels. As the basilica's overall iconographic program already comprised a Marian cycle, located in the small western vaults of the two transepts, the scenes in the new chapel amount to a sort of appendix.

At the top of the vault, a rectangular section decorated with shoots of flowering acanthus contains three tondi: the *Virgin and Child*, *David* and *Isaiah*. Thus the figure of Mary is presented here as the link between the Old Testament, represented by the two prophets, and the New Testament, embodied in the figure of the Christ Child, whom she is holding in her arms and showing to humanity as its Redeemer. David and Isaiah, with their prophecies of the Messiah, are placed alongside Mary several times in the basilica. The best-known examples are the figures at the center of the dome of the Prophets, above the presbytery, and the ones on the south wall of the nave, set in precious thirteenth-century *pinakes*.

The sequence of the five scenes begins on the left with the *Birth of Mary*, located inside a house in the Venetian Gothic style. Her mother Ann is shown lying on a bed in the background on the right, while two midwives bathe the newborn child under the affectionate gaze of her father Joachim. The scene is completed by a woman spinning on the left and two more women arriving on a visit from the right. A large

122 *facing page*

View of the Mascoli Chapel

The chapel is a perfect example of Gothic Renaissance architecture and decoration. On the splendid vault adorned with the most delicate mosaics in the basilica – made with tesserae as small as three millimeters a side – the Venetian school of Michele Giambono, with the *Birth of the Virgin* and the *Presentation in the Temple*, confronts the Tuscan one of Andrea del Castagno, with the *Visit to Saint Elizabeth* and the *Dormitio Virginis*. The former have architectural backdrops in the Gothic style, the latter in the Renaissance style.

peacock is perched in clear view on a balcony above, symbolizing resurrection and immortality.

Mary's *Presentation in the Temple*, in the second scene, is set on the threshold of a domed building on a central plan, again in the Venetian Gothic style. This has already been turned into a Christian church, as crosses are clearly recognizable on top of the small cupolas at the sides. An old priest greets the girl, who hands him a lighted candle. She is accompanied by her elderly parents and two women, one of whom is holding two white doves in her half-hidden hands, a traditional sacrificial offering.

In the lunette at the back, pierced by a richly decorated and highly symbolic circular window, the only source of light in the chapel, we see the *Annunciation* to Mary of the birth of her son Jesus, a light that will never set for humanity. The angel Gabriel is kneeling on the left, while Mary is seated at a desk on the right, busy reading the scriptures: the expression on her face and the gesture of her hand conveys her surprise at the events. In the middle, above the "eye" of light, God the Father is sending his Spirit down to Mary in the customary guise of a dove.

Moving on to the right-hand half of the tunnel vault, the novelty of the magnificent Renaissance architecture that frames the two last scenes is immediately apparent. This difference between the two sides of the vault has led to long debate among scholars over the reason why Michele Giambono, who signed the left-hand side, failed to complete the work, and over the hypothetical influence on the right-hand side of a Tuscan artist like Andrea del Castagno, who was present in Venice during that period.

Consequently, the "small" chapel has come to be seen as a "great" melting pot, bringing together the stimuli and ideas of many Venetian artists and *foresti* (artists from "outside"), and the right-hand half of the vault almost as a manifesto of the imminent architectural renovation of the city.

The first of the two scenes is the *Visitation* of Mary to Elizabeth, her elderly cousin who is expecting a son, the future John the Baptist. The embrace of the two women, standing by themselves at the center, powerfully expresses the intense feelings that prompted Mary to pronounce the *Magnificat*, the hymn of praise to God for the great things that he had done to her, as we read in the Gospel according to Luke (1, 46-55).

The Death of the Virgin, finally, in the presence of the twelve apostles, is a story from the Apocrypha that for centuries has formed the basis of this well-known iconographic type, associated with the idea of the immediate assumption of Mary into Heaven, where she is greeted after her death by her son Jesus, depicted in a mandorla of glory.

123

Scenes from the Life of the Virgin, Her Birth, mosaic, Mascoli Chapel

The detail shows the Gothic architecture of the mosaic; the typology of the transennas is characteristic.

THE PALA D'ORO AND THE TREASURY OF ST. MARK'S

Ettore Vio

The Treasury of St. Mark's houses a rich collection of objects made from gold, silver, precious and semiprecious stones, rock crystal and worked and painted glass, along with refined articles produced for the churches and palaces of Constantinople and the most elegant and precious creations that Venetian craftsmen were able to come up with in their desire to add to the glory of St. Mark's, seen as a metaphor for the Venetian duchy. It also contains examples of some of the most prestigious medieval and Renaissance art to have been produced in Western Europe.

The oldest part of the collection was formed after 1204, following the conquest of Byzantium and the creation of the Latin Empire of the East (1204-61) by the Crusaders, when many objects of sumptuary art were brought to Venice from the capital on the Bosphorus. It was further enriched with the conquest of Tyre and then with the abandonment of Candia (now Iraklion) by the Venetians, who sought to save as much of their valuable possessions as possible by taking them to Venice. Numerous precious gifts were also received from pontiffs and from the sovereigns of Western Europe.

Catastrophic fires like the one that broke out in 1231, or robberies like the one plotted in 1449 by the Greek Stamati Crassioti and then foiled by a "tip-off" from a friend, earning him the death penalty, put the Treasury to a severe test. With the fall of the republic, in 1797, it suffered what might have been a *coup de grâce* and was reduced to its current 283 pieces.

Of all these, the most venerated and loved by the Venetian people is the *Nikopoia* (an image of the Madonna that was believed to bring victory to embattled armies, where it was set up in the front lines to protect them against the enemy). It is an icon set in a frame of gilded silver, enamel and precious stones, painted by a Byzantine artist in the tenth century and inspired by a Madonna in mosaic located between the figures of Constantine and Justinian in the southern vestibule of Hagia Sophia in Constantinople. Its beauty was considered so divine that it was said to be *acheiropoietos*, i.e. not made by ordinary human hand, but by St. Luke who, through divine inspiration, painted the first ever picture of the Mother of God (held by some to be this very icon). Over the centuries it has accumulated a substantial amount of jewelry, now kept in a safe, testifying to the deep faith that the image has inspired.

But what is considered by all to be the most precious and refined gem in the collection, an expression of the

124
Pala d'oro

The *Golden Altarpiece* was ordered by Doge Ordelaffo Falier in 1102 and finished in Byzantium in 1105. Later enamels looted from Constantinople during the Fourth Crusade were added at the top. Originally set between two columns supporting statues of the Annunciation (now in the Treasury of St. Mark's), it bent backward at the top and was covered by a "ferial" altarpiece all year round except for feast days. The present structure, made by the goldsmith Giovanni Paolo Bonesegna (1345) has been sealed inside a protective case with a wheel mechanism that allows the front of the altarpiece to be turned to face the nave on special occasions. The rest of the time the altarpiece faces toward the back of the presbytery, where it can be admired by tourists, while the ferial altarpiece, a panel painting of the 15th century Venetian school, is visible from the altar. Two more ferial altarpieces were painted, the first by Paolo Veneziano in 1345 and the second by Maffeo da Verona in the 17th century, both of which are now in the museum.

125 *following pages*
Pala d'oro

The altarpiece, about three meters long and two meters high, is exceptionally rich, covered with precious stones, gold and enamels. It is composed of three different parts. In the lower central part, made in Byzantium (1102-05), the Prophets foretelling the Emmanuel to come are represented in three successive rows starting from the lower edge. At the center the Virgin, future Mother of God, flanked by Princess Irene and Doge Ordelaffo Falier, who replaces the earlier figure of a Comnenus, probably the basileus of Constantinople at the time the altarpiece was ordered. In the central row we see the Apostles with Christ enthroned in the middle and surrounded by the Evangelists. In the upper row the Archangels sing the glory of God, with the throne of the *Hetoimasia* in the middle. The upper part was made with *cloisonné* enamels looted during the Fourth Crusade. They represent six of the church's festivals (*Life of Christ and the Apostles*), with the archangel Michael, defender of the city and the church, at the center. It can be dated to the 10th century and is composed of the most splendid Byzantine enamels. A series of small panels with *Scenes from the History of the Church and the Life of Saint Mark* are set along the sides of the altarpiece, in the lower part and along the line dividing the two parts. The *cloisonné* enamels are made with gold leaf as a ground. Powdered glass was placed inside the cells formed by thin strips of gold and, after melting in the furnace, took on their definitive color, forming a continuous sheet about five millimeters thick through which the gold ground gleams. The enamels are set in gilded frames of various shapes, embellished with semiprecious stones.

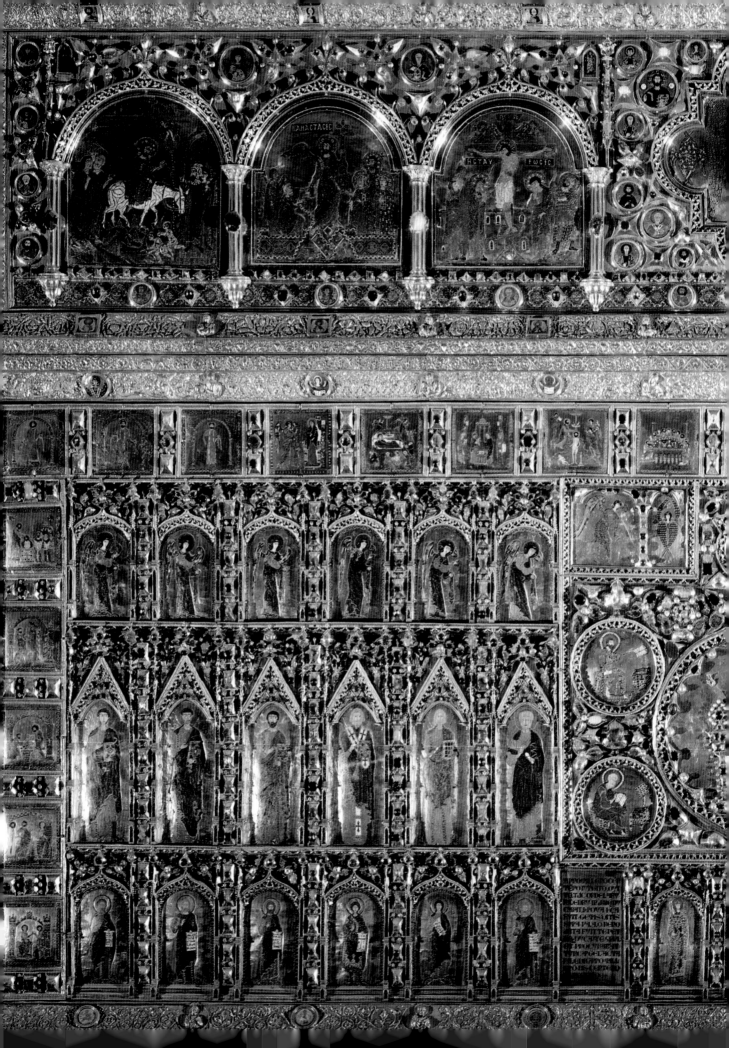

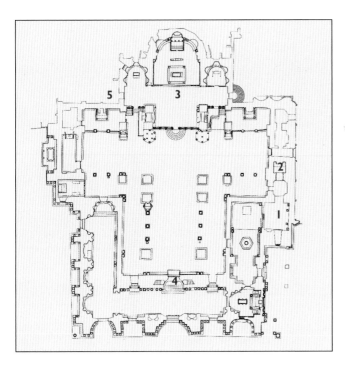

126

Plan of the basilica showing the route that has to be followed to reach the three areas used to house and display the basilica's various treasures.

At the end of the right-hand transept is set the entrance to the Treasury of St. Mark's (1), with objects brought back from the Fourth Crusade. These include famous works in rock crystal, glass vases, sardonyx amphorae, ampullae and bowls from Persia (Fatimid period, 9th–11th cent.), Byzantine icons of the Archangel Michael of the highest value and quality, with *cloisonné* enamels, Byzantine chalices made by goldsmith's workshops in the 9th–11th century and sardonyx goblets dating from the 1st–2nd century AD, candlesticks, crosiers, chalices from the Venetian Gothic period, articles made from rock crystal and filigree, the embossed and gilded silver *artoforion* in the form of a basilica and a whole series of other objects from different eras, including the golden rose given to Venice by a pope and the broadsword of Doge Francesco Morosini.

Next to the Treasury lies the sanctuary used for the conservation of relics (2). These include: Henry II's cross (1206–16), a relic of the True Cross, a case of gilded bronze containing a golden reliquary with the wood of Christ's cross, made by the French goldsmith Gerardo. From the chapel of St. Clement we can move on to the *Pala d'oro* (3), placed on the high altar.

At the sides of the central portal (4), in the atrium, along the staircase and in the museum above the narthex, where the chief exhibit is the four horses of St. Mark, we find cases containing mosaics that have been removed from the walls of the basilica and other objects in stone.

Emerging from the chapel of St. Peter and into the canon's courtyard, it is possible to take an elevator up to the museum in the Banquet Hall (5). Here we can admire the tapestries of the *Passion* (15th century), the tapestries with *Scenes from the Life of Saint Mark*, two ducal altar frontals (16th century), tapestries representing scenes of chivalry from Flanders (15th century), Byzantine veils (13th century, restored in the 19th century), shirts and blouses with Burano lace (second half of 17th century), ferial altarpieces by Paolo Veneziano (14th century) and Maffeo da Verona (17th century), internal and external organ doors decorated by Gentile Bellini (15th century), Giovan Battista Tiepolo's *Nativity of Christ* (18th century), the golden lion of the left-hand organ, the doge's throne and other objects.

metaphysical genius of Byzantium and of the cult of light, seen as a means of elevating human beings toward God and a fundamental element in Western Gothic culture, is the *Pala d'oro*, or *Golden Altarpiece*, set on the high altar of St. Mark's Basilica and glorifying the evangelist whose relics lie beneath. The enamels, executed at Constantinople in 1105 to a commission by Doge Ordelaffo Falier, were framed at the time in such a way that the square panels, now arranged vertically at the sides of the altarpiece, were lined up at the base to tell the *Story of Saint Mark*. The other square panels, with *Scenes from the Life of Christ*, now set horizontally in the fourth row from the bottom, were originally located above the other plaquettes with scenes from the life of the evangelist so as to represent the *Gospel according to Saint Mark*, an indispensable means of gaining access to the heavenly city depicted above. This predella made up of two rows of panels of *cloisonné* enamel constituted a sort of prologue to the vision of Paradise above. The center of the altarpiece is dominated by the figure of Christ enthroned, while his word is revealed by the four evangelists, laid out around him inside *clipei*, or round shields, and the twelve apostles (six of them lined up to the left of the Omnipotent and six to the right). The coming of the Son of God is predicted in the lower level, underneath the apostles, by twelve prophets (six to the left and six to the right of the central figure of the praying Virgin, flanked by the rulers of Venice and Byzantium and by plaques with inscriptions recounting the history of the altarpiece itself). Above Christ at the center we see the Throne ready for the second coming of God on earth and reserved for the Last Judgment, adored by a line of cherubim, angels and archangels in the third row.

The large frieze at the top, which comes from one of the three churches of the Constantinopolitan monastery, or monastery of the Pantocrator, with the Archangel Michael in the middle and six panels depicting the *Entry of Christ into Jerusalem, Descent into Limbo, Crucifixion, Ascension, Pentecost* and *Death of the Virgin* were added to the altarpiece in 1209. In 1345 it was completed by the goldsmith Giovanni Paolo Bonesegna, with the addition of many precious stones and the new Gothic frame commissioned from him by the procurator Andrea Dandolo, who later became doge. A total of 1927 gems are mounted on it: 526 pearls, 330 garnets, 320 emeralds, 255 sapphires, 183 amethysts, 75 rubies, 175 agates, 34 topazes, 16 cornelians and 13 jaspers. The *cloisonné* enamels of the Gothic frame, with their precious colors set inside the gold wire that borders the cells, into which they were poured in a liquid state, perform the same function, that of emphasizing the abstract qualities of the light, as the stained glass placed in the windows of cathedrals. The result is a perfect fusion between a material of exclusively Byzantine origin (enamel) and the more exclusive creation of the Western sensibility (Gothic architecture), based on the manipulation of light. The metaphysical qualities of the light in the enamel panels are combined with the anagogic ones (of mystical elevation to God) of the new Gothic framing. The image of the altarpiece is that of the Heavenly Jerusalem, transformed into a metaphor of Venice at a moment when it seemed predestined to inherit the mantle of capital of the Eastern Roman empire, which God had chosen as the seat for his Church, transferred by Constantine from Rome to Byzantium.

In addition to such precious and venerated reliquaries as those of Christ's Blood, the Wood of the Cross, the Pillar of the Flagellation and the Sacred Purple, one of the most extraordinary objects in the Treasury, for its light and color, is the icon with a bust of the Archangel Michael (tenth-eleventh century), in which the face, forearms and hands are all in gilded silver. The wings, halo and sleeves are made from *cloisonné* enamel, while the *loros* (a band around the bust) is studded with gems. The other icon representing the Archangel Michael dressed as a warrior against a background decorated entirely with enamel, as is his cuirass, dates from the following century. Here the decorative and chromatic fantasy of the goldsmith seems inexhaustible and aimed at the greatest possible abstraction of the image.

127

Doge Ordelaffo Falier, Pala d'oro, detail

In the present organization of the altarpiece, due to the goldsmith Giovanni Paolo Bonesegna (1345), plaquettes representing Princess Irene and the doge are set in the lower row, to the right and left of the Blessed Virgin in an attitude of prayer. As an examination of the material has shown that the doge's head is a replacement, it has been suggested that prior to the Fourth Crusade it had represented a basileus of Constantinople, probably the princess's husband. After the breakdown of relations with the Byzantines, it appears that the Venetians decided to substitute the head of the doge who had ordered the altarpiece from Constantinople in 1102.

Outstanding among the chalices is that of the Roman emperor, with a sardonyx bowl carved into stylized petals (first century AD) and a support of Byzantine silver gilt (tenth century). Plaquettes of *cloisonné* enamel, bordered by rows of pearls and depicting Christ, the Virgin, John the Baptist, Peter, Paul, the Evangelists, the Doctors and the Archangels, have the role of sanctifying the chalice and guaranteeing the invocation "May the Lord aid the Roman Orthodox Emperor" written in Greek on the upper edge of the precious support. If it was ever used in Communion, the reddish-brown colors of the sardonyx must have given the impression, when it was lifted and viewed against the light, that it contained the Precious Blood that was shed for the salvation of humanity. In fact

symbolism and abstraction were the ultimate goals of
Byzantine aesthetics and the craftsmen who drew their
inspiration from it. The same effect is produced by another
chalice in sardonyx with handles (first century AD), supported
by a stem and ringed by a border that are both made of silver
gilt and Byzantine *cloisonné* enamels representing Christ,
the Virgin, John the Baptist, Archangels, Apostles, Doctors,
Bishops, Deacons and Martyrs. Under the base of the cup is
set the Greek inscription: "May the Lord aid the Roman
Orthodox Emperor" (tenth century).

If these two chalices are the most precious and the ones
with the deepest symbolic meaning for the celebration of
the Eucharist (although they were probably never used at
St. Mark's), the small temple of openwork silver gilt with a
square and quatrefoil plan, five cupolas and four pinnacles
topped by crosses was originally used to hold the Eucharistic
bread (*artoforion*). This function is illustrated by the
iconographic theme represented on the curved surfaces of the
casket (formerly thought to be a perfume burner) with
elements depicting the *Garden of Eden* and the *Tree of Life* at
the top, while the fantastic animals on the base allude to the
Vices, overcome by Courage and Prudence, embodied by the
figures of a warrior and a woman with Greek inscriptions on
the doors. In fact it is these two virtues that permit entry into
the temple and access to the Eucharist.

In any case the refinement of the engraving and
embossing, in combination with the gilding that runs along
the edges and corners and covers the allegorical figures and
with the architectural elements (exedras, spires, domes and
domed lantern), results in an object of totally abstract form,
whose meaning is only comprehensible in a metaphysical
dimension.

128 *preceding pages*

**Christ the Pantocrator,
Pala d'oro, detail**

The detail showing Christ the
Pantocrator, surrounded by the
Evangelists, presents enamels of the
highest quality. It is set in the
central row of the original panel of
the altarpiece ordered by Falier.

129

**The Archangel Michael,
"standing" and embossed,
Treasury of St. Mark's.**

Icon in *cloisonné* enamels on gold
and precious stones. Byzantine
gold work from the end of the
11th century. At the sides we can
see pairs of warrior saints in
enameled medallions, identified
by inscriptions.

130 *above*

Paolo Veneziano and sons, Ferial Altarpiece, 1345

The first and most important "weekday covering" of the *Pala d'oro*. It is a wooden panel with two levels of paintings: the upper one represents Christ and the Virgin between Saints Theodore, Mark, John the Evangelist, Peter and Nicholas; the lower one, *Scenes from the Life of Saint Mark*.

132 *right*

Greek artoforion, 12th-century silver work, Treasury of St. Mark's

A reliquary in the form of a small domed church, made out of silver and partially gilded, it dates from the end of the 12th century. It was originally used to hold the Eucharistic bread.

131 *facing page*

Chalice of the Patriarchs, Byzantine gold work, 10th century, Treasury of St. Mark's

Decorated with silver gilt, *cloisonné* enamels and pearls, the chalice is made out of a block of variegated sardonyx. The mounting is typical of the Byzantine era, when goblets dating from the early centuries of Christianity were reutilized.

172

THE TAPESTRIES

Maria Da Villa Urbani

One of the chief delights of the museum of St. Mark's Basilica is its collection of fifteenth- and sixteenth-century tapestries. Recently subjected to comprehensive restoration, they have regained their original beauty, allowing us to appreciate once again the perfection of the ancient workmanship and the preciosity of the materials, rescued from the damage wrought by the passage of time and the effects of clumsy restorations carried out over the course of the centuries.

In addition to the fragments that come from the bequest of Cardinal Giovanni Battista Zen, the four pieces of woolen cloth figured with *Scenes from the Passion of Jesus*, originally used for religious services in Holy Week, also date from the fifteenth century. The thirteen scenes, from the *Last Supper* to the *Appearance to the Apostles in the Presence of Thomas*, are set in ten panels framed by plant borders. The symbol of the lion *in moleca*, or in the form of a stylized crab, recurs frequently, underlining the fact that the images were woven for Venetian clients. The cartoons for these tapestries, executed in the flourishing factories of Arras in the early part of the fifteenth century, have recently been firmly attributed by art historians to the Venetian Niccolò di Pietro.

The four tapestries with *Scenes from the Life of Saint Mark* and the two votive altar frontals of Doge Alvise Mocenigo (1571, to a cartoon by Jacopo Tintoretto) and Marino Grimani (1595, to a cartoon by Domenico Tintoretto) were made during the sixteenth century. All the sixteenth-century tapestries were woven in Florence and are characterized by the use of extremely precious and delicate yarn, such as silk and gold and silver thread. The series of *Scenes from the Life of Saint Mark*, depicting the miracles he worked, including the famous one of the healing of the cobbler Anian, and his martyrdom, was commissioned by the procurators of St. Mark from the Florentine tapestry factory, directed by the Fleming Giovanni Rost, on October 20, 1550, to decorate the sides of the presbytery. The statement in the contract that the tapestries were to be woven to a design that "will be sent by Master Jacobo Sansovino," *proto* of St. Mark's at the time, meant that the cartoons were long thought to have been produced by Sansovino, but recently critics have tended to see their style as having greater affinities with works by Andrea Schiavone or Giuseppe Porta called Salviati.

Two other textiles in the basilica's museum are among the finest antique examples of the use of gold and silk embroidery for altar paraments to have come out of the workshops of Byzantium and can be dated to the twelfth or thirteenth century. The first is decorated with the figures of Archangels Michael and Gabriel, while the other represents the dead Christ, watched over by two angels and surrounded by symbols of the evangelists.

133

Tapestries of the Passion, detail of the scene of the Deposition, Museum of St. Mark's

The tapestries of the Passion, made outside Italy to cartoons by a Venetian painter in the first quarter of the 15th century, are the most important woolen hangings in the country. They consist of four separate pieces, two of them with three scenes and two with just two.

ESSENTIAL BIBLIOGRAPHY

1604
Venetia città nobilissima et singolare descritta già in XIIII. libri da M. Francesco Sansovino et hora con molta diligenza corretta, emendata, e più d'un terzo di cose nuove ampliata dal M.R.D. Giovanni Stringa. Venice.

1888-1892
La basilica di San Marco in Venezia, illustrata nella storia e nell'arte da scrittori veneziani, edited by Camillo Boito, Ferdinando Ongania Editore. Venice.

1944
SERGIO BETTINI, *I mosaici antichi di San Marco a Venezia.* Bergamo.

1946
SERGIO BETTINI, *L'architettura di San Marco: origini e significato.* Padua.

1960
OTTO DEMUS, *The Church of San Marco in Venice: History, Architecture, Sculpture.* Washington.

1965-1971
Il tesoro di San Marco: I. La Pala d'oro - II. Il tesoro e il museo, edited by Hans R. Hahnloser. Florence- Venice.

1975
FERDINANDO FORLATI, *La basilica di San Marco attraverso i suoi restauri.* Trieste.

1983
WLADIMIRO DORIGO, *Venezia origini: fondamenti, ipotesi, metodo.* Milan.

1984
OTTO DEMUS, *The Mosaics of San Marco in Venice.* Chicago and London.

1986
I mosaici di San Marco: iconografia dell'Antico e del Nuovo Testamento, edited by Bruno Bertoli. Milan.

1990
Basilica patriarcale in Venezia. San Marco: i mosaici, la storia, l'illuminazione, edited by Ettore Vio. Milan.

1991
Basilica patriarcale in Venezia, San Marco: i mosaici, le iscrizioni, la pala d'oro, edited by Ettore Vio. Milan.

1991
RENATO POLACCO, *San Marco: la basilica d'oro.* Milan.

1992-1993
Basilica patriarcale in Venezia: San Marco: I. La cripta, la storia, la conservazione – II. La cripta, il restauro, edited by Ettore Vio. Milan.

1993
La basilica di San Marco: arte e simbologia, edited by Bruno Bertoli, Milan.

1994
ANTONIO NIERO, *San Marco: la vita e i mosaici.* Venice.

1995
Le sculture esterne di San Marco, edited by Wolfgang Wolters. Milan.

1996
San Marco: aspetti storici e agiografici. Atti del convegno internazionale di studi, Venezia 26-29 aprile 1994, edited by Antonio Niero. Venice.

1997
Storia dell'arte marciana: I. L'architettura – II. I mosaici – III. Sculture, tesoro, arazzi. Atti del convegno internazionale di studi, Venezia 11-14 ottobre 1994, edited by Renato Polacco. Venice.

1999
Scienza e tecnica del restauro della basilica. Atti del convegno internazionale di studi, Venezia 16-19 maggio 1995, edited by Ettore Vio and Antonio Lepschy. Venice.